RVing Basics

RVing Basics

Bill and Jan Moeller

Ragged Mountain Press
Camden, Maine

International Marine/
Ragged Mountain Press

A Division of The McGraw·Hill Companies

10 9 8

Copyright © 1995 Bill and Jan Moeller.
All rights reserved. The publisher takes no responsibility for the use of any of the
materials or methods described in this book, nor for the products thereof. The name
"Ragged Mountain Press" and the Ragged Mountain Press logo are trademarks of
The McGraw-Hill Companies. Printed in the United States of America.

Library of Congress Cataloging-in-Publication Data

Moeller, Bill, 1930-
    RVing basics / Bill and Jan Moeller.
        p.   cm
    Includes index.
    ISBN 0-07-042779-8
        1. Mobile home living—United states.   I. Moeller, Jan, 1930-
    II. Title.
    TX1107.M67   1995
    796.7'9 — dc20   94-39885
                                                          CIP

Questions regarding the content of this
book should be addressed to:
Ragged Mountain Press
P.O. Box 220
Camden, ME 04843
207-236-4837

Questions regarding the ordering of this
book should be addressed to:
The McGraw-Hill Companies
Customer Service Department
P.O. Box 547
Blacklick, OH 43004
Retail customers: 1-800-262-4729
Bookstores: 1-800-722-4726

A portion of the profits from the sale of each
Ragged Mountain Press book is donated to an environmental cause.

RVing Basics is printed on 60-pound Renew Opaque Vellum, an acid-free paper
that contains 50 percent recycled waste paper (preconsumer)
and 10 percent postconsumer waste paper.

Photographs and illustrations are by the authors, unless otherwise credited.
Printed by Quebecore Printing, Fairfield, PA
Design by Eugenie S. Delaney
Production by Dan Kirchoff
Edited by Jonathan Eaton, Constance Burt, and Pamela Benner

Contents

Preface

Many years ago, when we began RVing, there were no books to tell us how. What we didn't learn by trial and error, we learned from seasoned RVers willing to share their knowledge. It took a long time for us to become fully conversant with all aspects of RVing.

This book is a compilation of what we have learned. All facets of RVing are included, from advice on the initial purchase of an RV and information on how to use it, to storing it between trips. Systems and equipment for every type of RV are covered, as are procedures for using the systems when on the road, when primitive camping, and when staying in campgrounds with all the amenities.

We designed the book as a reference work to help RVers—beginners and experienced—avoid pitfalls so they can enjoy trouble-free RVing and the RV lifestyle to its fullest.

Acknowledgments

This book would not be as complete as it is without the help of countless RVers who have given us valuable tips and advice over the years. Our RVing friends will recognize what they have contributed; so, too, perhaps, will those anonymous RVers we have observed and from whom we have learned much. To all of you, known and unknown, our thanks.

We are grateful to the many manufacturers of RVs and RV equipment who so enthusiastically supplied an abundance of photographs and illustrations. We deeply appreciate your cooperation.

Special thanks to Ryan Jones of Viking Trailer Sales in Newport, Oregon, and to the managers of Pacific Shores and Whaler's Rest campgrounds, who allowed us to roam through their facilities to take photographs.

Excellent editorial and technical advice and attention to detail were provided by the consummate professionals at Ragged Mountain Press: Jonathan Eaton, Pamela Benner, and Dan Kirchoff, along with Constance Burt and Hyman Rudoff. It was a pleasure working with you all.

And special thanks to Bonnie Jensen, without whose help our traveling lifestyle wouldn't run nearly so smoothly.

Chapter 1

An Overview of RVing

Nearly everyone knows what a recreational vehicle (RV) is, but those who haven't owned or used one may have no idea of what RVing entails; if they have any ideas, they are often based on supposition, not fact, and may tend to be negative. Let us dispel some of the misconceptions about RVing.

RVing Is Not Roughing It

Me? RV? No thanks. I don't want anything to do with it. This is the attitude of some people who don't want to become involved with RVing because they associate RVs with roughing it. Undoubtedly this is because some RV terminology gives a false impression of what RVing is: RVs are usually taken to a campsite in a campground, and this activity is called camping. The word "camp," in any of its forms, often brings to mind living and cooking in primitive conditions, battling insects, and, when the weather is not ideal, being cold, or wet, or hot. If that is what camping connotes to you, you are probably influenced by what it used to be. Things have changed: Today's RVers can set up camp in the most remote spot and be almost as comfortable as they would be at home.

Even the smallest trailers and motorhomes—15 to 20 feet long—have standing headroom and are equipped with many conveniences: an enclosed bath with toilet, lavatory, and shower; a galley featuring a three- or four-burner range, often with an oven; a propane/electric refrigerator with freezer; hot and cold running water; a dinette; sleeping accommodations for four or more, including a double or queen-size bed or optional twin beds; a wardrobe; and plenty of cabinets for storing necessities.

In addition, RVs are equipped with screened windows and roof vents, numerous electric lights and receptacles for operating electrical equipment, and probably a thermostat-controlled furnace. An air conditioner can be added to most RVs, if desired.

Each RV unit is attractively decorated with coordinated draperies, upholstery, and floor coverings. It may be carpeted or have an easy-care vinyl floor covering, and it may have mini-blinds or pleated shades on the windows in addition to draperies.

All trailers and motorhomes have a built-in tank for fresh water, and nearly all recently manufactured units have built-in holding tanks for collecting waste. Water from the sinks and the shower drains into a gray-water holding tank; toilet waste is flushed into a black-water holding tank. This arrangement enables you to use your own private toilet and shower facilities, just as you do at home, no matter where you are camped. Doing without showers or trekking to a pit toilet will not be a concern. Even if the RV is parked in a campground with full hookups at your site, with holding tanks you are free from the inconvenience of using public toilets and showers.

Figure 1-1. *This Prowler conventional trailer features a completely equipped front galley, living room, full bath, and rear bedroom. The rear bed may be either a queen or a double. Other sleeping accommodations include a convertible sofa and dinette.* (Courtesy Fleetwood Enterprises, Inc.)

Figure 1-2. *The view toward the front of a Tioga Montara 27-foot Class C motorhome. A roomy bunk is over the cab, the dinette converts into a bed, and the rear bedroom is furnished with a double bed, two wardrobes, and many overhead cabinets. A spacious full bath is located just in front of the rear bedroom.* (Courtesy Fleetwood Enterprises, Inc.)

If you dislike the dried or canned foods that are a camping tradition, you'll never have to eat them if you have an RV. You won't have to cook over a campfire—unless you want to—or use an awkward camp stove or contend with a messy ice chest. The modern RV galley allows you to cook and prepare foods exactly as you do at home. Plenty of cabinets are available for food storage; fresh vegetables, meats, and beverages can be kept cold in the refrigerator. Casseroles, pizza, desserts, and breadstuffs can be baked in the oven. Foods can be prepared at home and stored in the RV's freezer so you can spend less vacation time in the galley.

The refrigerator, water heater, galley range, and furnace run on propane gas supplied from the one or two gas cylinders with which all RVs are equipped.

The lights in the RV operate on 12-volt direct current and are powered by the RV's batteries. Certain appliances, such as TVs, razors, hair curlers, fans, mixers, and coffeemakers in 12-volt versions, can also be run off the batteries. The batteries provide power for the water pump, which pumps water from the built-in tank to the faucets, so pressurized running water is always available.

Wrestling with a sleeping bag is not necessary. An RV bed is equipped with an innerspring mattress that takes standard sheets and blankets.

If you have avoided RVing because you thought it was too much like camping out or roughing it, it's time to rethink your position. Any one of today's modern, comfortable RVs can truly be a home away from home, whether it is parked in an isolated spot with no hookups or in the most luxurious campground with full hookups.

RVing Takes No Special Skills

No special skills are needed for RVing. Anyone who drives an automobile can handle a motorhome or a tow vehicle pulling a trailer (most problems with trailer towing are due to improper hitching, not shortcomings of the driver). The driver is immediately conscious of the length of the RV and automatically compensates for it when turning and passing, and quickly adjusts to the extra weight involved when stopping. Except in extreme circumstances, that's all there is to driving or towing an RV.

Backing a trailer is a worry for some, but anyone can learn with a little practice. That's how trailerists learn—by practicing.

Hitching may seem complicated, but about 10 minutes of instruction is all it takes to explain the process. It's that simple.

Nothing about setting up or breaking camp with an RV requires any more physical strength or agility than most people possess. To avoid any sort of exertion, however, RVers have the option of equipping their rigs with all types of electric and hydraulic aids.

RVing Isn't Only for the Able-bodied

What about those who don't have normal strength or agility? Wouldn't RVing be difficult or impossible for them? The answer is no. These days RVing isn't confined to the able-bodied; those with disabilities can participate fully in nearly all aspects of RVing.

Most public campgrounds have a site or two reserved for the handi-

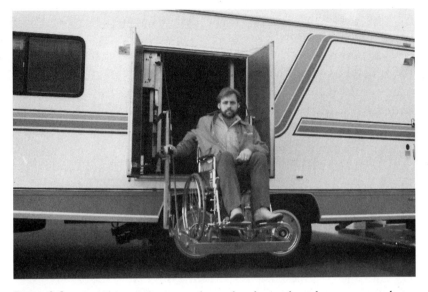

Figure 1-3. *The door on this motorhome has been altered to accommodate a wheelchair lift.* (Courtesy Foretravel of Texas, Inc.)

capped, as do some private campgrounds, and it is quite likely that a handicap-accessible restroom will be available.

Of course, a campsite won't be of much use to those with disabilities unless they can get to it in a suitable RV. For many years it has been possible to adapt automobiles and trucks for drivers with disabilities, but RV manufacturers have only recently begun to adapt their units for special needs. In addition to these manufacturers are numerous companies that make devices of all types to aid disabled RVers.

As a matter of fact, the best way for the handicapped to vacation may well be in an RV; indeed, for some, an RV is an ideal dwelling to live in fulltime. When traveling, there is never the worry about finding an accessible public toilet; your own is always right there with you. And once you are inside a motorhome or a conventional trailer, the floor is level, without any steps to negotiate. Perhaps walkers, canes, or crutches could be dispensed with inside the RV. Unlike a typical house, an RV has no 20- or 30-foot-long rooms with vast open walkways. The total living area of even the largest RVs is a maximum of 8½ feet wide by about 40 feet long, so each room is just a few feet away from the others. Given the narrow walkways, there are always counters, tabletops, and other handholds within reach for support or steadying. A disabled person may find it much easier to get around in an RV than in a house or apartment.

A disability is rarely a valid reason in itself for being unable to enjoy RVing, and many of the handicapped look upon RVing as a release from confinement. They will do whatever it takes to enjoy the freedom that RVing makes possible. On numerous occasions we have seen RVers with physical disabilities—some confined to wheelchairs—using ramps and lifts to enter and exit their RVs.

Those with an infirmity or disability shouldn't let it dissuade them from RVing until they have investigated the possibilities. Handicapped RVers or those who would like to become RVers may want to join the Handicapped Travel Club (dues are $3 a year), 4500 Tennessee Avenue, Chattanooga, Tennessee 37409. The Recreation Vehicle Industry Association (RVIA) offers a free leaflet titled "RV Accessibility for the Handicapped," which lists RV manufacturers that custom-build or adapt their units for the handicapped. Write to RVIA, Department RVT, Box 2999, Reston, Virginia 22090-0999; 703-620-6003.

The Economy and Convenience of Traveling by RV

If you want to save money when traveling, RVing is the way to do it. A recent study compared RV vacations with those involving other modes of transportation. For a family of four, RV trips cost 50 percent less than traveling by car with overnight stays in hotels or motels, and 75 percent less than air/hotel/motel vacations. Among eight vacation types, the four most economical were trips on which an RV was used—regardless of distance of the trip, how long it lasted, and in what region of the United States it took place.

RV traveling can't be beat for convenience. No packing, unpacking, or living out of a suitcase is necessary—clothes and toiletries are always handy. Finding decent restaurants isn't a problem—meals can be easily prepared in the RV's galley. Snacks and beverages are readily available too. Perhaps most important, expenses for eating out can be eliminated from the vacation budget.

Let's say that during a day's run, the kids want to cool off on a water slide. You park the RV nearby, the kids don swimwear, and have their fun. You prepare lunch in the galley while they change back into traveling clothes, and then you resume the trip.

Because they are self-contained, RVs are especially convenient when Mother Nature acts up. One night found us parked in a campground in a small town in North Carolina during a severe winter storm. With the high winds and drenching rain, it wasn't long before all the electricity in town went out. Everything was black, except our trailer—we happened to be the only RV in the campground. For our lights, we were using the RV's battery-powered, 12-volt, direct-current electrical system. The furnace also operates on 12 volts, but to avoid running down the battery, we switched to our propane catalytic heater for warmth. Nothing in our refrigerator or freezer was affected by the power outage because the propane switched on automatically when the electricity went out. We had ample water supply from our internal tank, and we prepared normal meals using the food we always have on hand. Electricity wasn't restored until late the next afternoon. We suspect that we fared better through it all than anyone else in town.

Those traveling in RVs would fare just as well if roads became impassable—from snow or flooding perhaps—and they had to pull off the road or into a rest area until they could resume the trip. We know of several people who have waited out such delays in the comfort of their RVs.

We have experienced two earthquakes in our trailer—both mild enough that little damage was done to the areas where we were staying. But even in a strong earthquake, RVs have no heavy structural members that could collapse, plaster won't fall from the walls, electric wires won't be wrenched out, and gas and water lines won't rupture. RVs are built to withstand the shaking and jolts of highway driving. Because it is spring-mounted, an RV is virtually earthquake-proof—as far as the shaking is concerned. After a quake, those who have RVs can use them as temporary shelters if their regular residences are damaged.

During a trip, if you hear warnings of expected severe weather or flooding, you may be able to avoid the storm simply by driving away. We escaped one of the worst snowstorms in a decade because we moved out of the storm's path. Another time, a hurricane threatened the coastal area where we were staying, so we moved inland to a safer place.

RV Nomenclature

RVing has a language all its own, and it's helpful to know some of the correct terminology. This section describes all types of RVs and

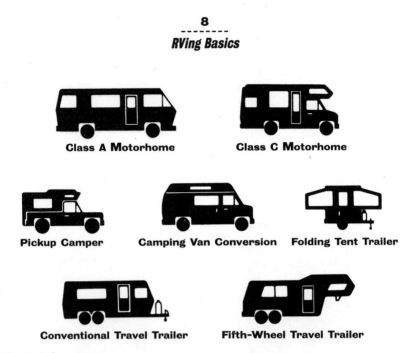

Figure 1-4. *Silhouettes of common RV types.* (Courtesy Recreation Vehicle Industry Association)

common RVing equipment and accessories (discussed at length in later chapters).

RV, of course, is the acronym for *recreational vehicle,* and describes motorhomes, travel trailers, folding tent trailers, pickup campers, and camping van conversions. (See Chapter 2 for photographs of each type of RV.)

Motorhomes and *camping van conversions* are self-propelled by an engine. *Trailers,* or *towables,* which do not have an engine, must be pulled by a *tow vehicle,* usually a pickup truck; passenger cars, vans, and sport utility vehicles are often used as tow vehicles as well. *Pickup campers,* or *slide-in* or *truck campers,* are installed in the bed of a pickup truck.

The cover for the bed of a pickup truck has different names in different parts of the country: *cap, shell, canopy,* or *topper;* we refer to it as a cap.

A motorhome is categorized as either *Class A, Class C* (sometimes called a *mini-motorhome*), *low-profile,* or *micro-mini.* Class A models and smaller low-profile motorhomes are somewhat box shaped and resemble buses, although many are sleeker and more streamlined. Class A motorhomes are about 11 feet tall; low-profile models are 8 or 9 feet tall. Some of the largest motorhomes are *bus conversions;* the chassis, frame, and engine of a bus are used as the basis for this type of

motorhome. Class C models are built on van chassis and have a cabover bunk; micro-minis are smaller versions of the Class C models. A larger motorhome is often referred to as a *coach*.

A camping van conversion (*Class B motorhome* is a less common name) is, as the name implies, a van from an automobile manufacturer that has been converted into an RV by removing some of the seats and installing sleeping accommodations, a tiny galley, dining table, storage areas, a toilet (in some), and, usually, a raised roof.

Figure 1-5. *A slideout is retracted for traveling but, when extended as shown, provides extra interior room.*

Two basic types of travel trailers are manufactured: conventional and fifth-wheel (a *fifth-wheel trailer* is sometimes called a "fiver"). Most *conventional trailers* have a boxlike configuration, but a fifth-wheel has an elevated front (the *gooseneck*) that projects over the bed of the pickup-truck tow vehicle. Under the front of the gooseneck, in the center, is the *kingpin box*.

A *slideout* is a section of the RV that extends about 3 feet beyond the normal width of a unit, enlarging the interior floor space (Figure 1-5). Slideouts are most common on fifth-wheel trailers, but some conventional trailers and motorhomes have this option.

Included in the travel trailer category are *telescoping trailers*. They look like conventional trailers until they are readied for traveling. Then, the top half of the trailer is lowered over the bottom half, resulting in a low-profile trailer (Figure 1-6).

Another type of trailer is the *folding tent trailer* on which the fabric, tentlike top portion folds down for towing. When set up, the top is raised to provide standing headroom, and the front and rear ends are unfolded, projecting outward from the body of the trailer to form roomy double berths.

A *basement model* RV has the living quarters above huge storage

Figure 1-6. *A Hi-Lo telescoping trailer ready for travel. When the top portion is raised, the headroom is 6 feet, 6 inches. (Courtesy Hi-Lo Trailer Company)*

areas along its length, some of which can run across the full width of the unit.

A trailer is attached to its tow vehicle with a *hitch*. The *kingpin* of a fifth-wheeler fits into a hitch in the bed of a pickup truck (see Figure 6-6, page 118); the kingpin is considered the "fifth-wheel," from which their name is derived. The hitch for a small conventional trailer is often nothing more than a ball attached to the bumper of the tow vehicle. A larger conventional trailer has a hitch with the ball mounted on a square shaft—a *draw bar*—which fits into a *receiver*— a steel framework bolted to the chassis of the tow vehicle. Unless the trailer is very small, the hitch should be a *weight-distributing,* or *load-equalizing,* type with *spring bars* that distribute the load between the front and rear wheels of the tow vehicle (see Figure 6-4, page 116). Larger trailers should have a *sway-control bar* for damping side-to-side motion while towing (see Figure 6-5, page 117).

A *stone shield,* or *rock guard*—a rigid, awninglike fiberglass or Lexan cover that can be raised or lowered—is found on the front and per-haps the back windows of trailers (Figure 1-7). (Some manufacturers refer to these as *awnings* in their brochures.)

Earlier we mentioned the two types of holding tanks found on most RVs: the *gray-water tank,* which collects shower and sink water, and the *black-water tank* for toilet waste. An RV so equipped is said to be *self-contained.*

Many RVs have a *monitor panel* with lights that indicate the water- and holding-tank levels, as well as the state of charge of the battery.

Figure 1-7. *A stone shield, when raised as shown, shades the window below and affords some protection from rain. Lowered for travel, it shields a trailer's front window from flying rocks.*

Figure 1-8. *Many municipalities have public dump stations, the locations of which are indicated by a blue-and-white sign with a trailer and sewer hose icon.*

Often the monitor panel is incorporated into the range hood.

In a campground or RV park, a *full-hookup* site has water, electricity, and a sewer drain into which the holding tanks can be emptied. Holding tanks also may be emptied at *dump stations.* Even if a campground has sites with sewers, a dump station may also be on the premises. Dump stations are also found in rest areas in some states, and at certain service stations, truckstops, and city parks (Figure 1-8).

Staying in a place with no hookups is known as *boondocking, primitive camping,* or *dry camping.* Many nautical terms are used in RVing. The kitchen is a *galley;* a campsite's electric hookup is often referred to as *shore power. Docking lights,* usually found on motorhomes, are bright exterior lights used for parking in the dark. *Cockpit* is the name often used for the driver/passenger area. And a car towed behind a motorhome may be called an *auxiliary vehicle* or a *dinghy;* however, a boat towed behind is called a boat. Dinghy towing is done with either a *tow bar* or a *tow dolly.*

To distinguish the left and right sides of an RV, the self-explanatory terms *curb side* and *street side* are used.

Even RVers themselves have special names. Those who live year-round in their RV are *fulltimers.* Those who travel by themselves are *loners.* When fulltimers, or any other RVers, go south for the winter, they turn into *snowbirds.*

Chapter 2

Choosing an RV

S electing the best RV for your purposes depends on many factors: how much money you can spend, how many people will sleep in it, where it will be used, and what type—trailer, motorhome, pickup camper, folding tent trailer, or camping van conversion—is the most suitable for your purposes.

An important but often overlooked consideration when contemplating the purchase of an RV is: Do you have a place to park the RV when you are not using it? If local ordinances preclude your parking the RV on the street, or if there is no suitable place to park it at your residence, you may have to keep it in a storage facility. This is a substantial additional expense that should be considered.

Other expenses are registration fees and insurance costs. Motorhomes, because they have an engine, cost more to register than trailers, and insurance for a motorhome is roughly 20 to 30 percent higher than for a trailer of the same length.

A Small or Large RV?

For many RVers, the money they can spend has a direct bearing on the size of the RV they can purchase. Even if cost isn't a factor, you shouldn't necessarily purchase a large unit just because you can afford one. RV buyers should purchase the size that best serves their needs. (Typical price ranges for all types of RVs are discussed later in this chapter.)

Except for very small or special-purpose RVs, small motorhomes around 20 feet long and travel trailers 15 to 20 feet long have all the basic equipment: sleeping accommodations for four; a galley with a range and often an oven, a sink, and a refrigerator/freezer; a dining table; a water heater; a furnace; one or two propane cylinders; 12- and

120-volt electrical systems; an enclosed area for the toilet; and adequate storage space. Units only a few feet longer usually have more sleeping accommodations; a bedroom with a folding or sliding door for privacy; a living room; and a bath with toilet, lavatory, and shower. As units increase in length, they usually have proportionately more storage space, roomier baths, a dinette, space for a sofa and one or two chairs in the living room, and, depending on the model, more sleeping accommodations.

Different people do different things with an RV, so the purposes for which it will be used, how often it will be used, and where it will be taken must be considered when deciding on its size. Will it be used mainly on weekends and taken to destinations close by? Will these places be primitive campgrounds or campgrounds with hookups? Or will it be used frequently for traveling long distances, or moved seasonally—that is, only twice a year or so?

Large RVs can't be maneuvered on the narrow, sharply curved roads typical of many primitive campgrounds, and they may not fit into any of the sites. RVers whose camping is mainly primitive should select a small unit, one that is self-contained with holding tanks for black and gray water and a freshwater tank. All tanks should have adequate capacity for the length of the intended stays in primitive campgrounds.

Those who don't travel a lot, using their RVs primarily for living quarters during extended stays in one place, could logically purchase the largest RV their budget allows. Opting for a size just big enough for your needs is more cost-effective if the trailer is used infrequently.

Large RVs are limited as to where they can safely be taken. To avoid low clearances, sharp curves, steep grades, and other obstacles, they must be driven on interstate highways, freeways, and main highways— the routes suitable for trucks.

If you will put a lot of miles on your RV, you will have more flexibility when traveling if your rig is not too long. The shorter the rig, the easier it is finding parking spaces at shopping centers and restaurants, as well as maneuvering in traffic and refueling. Smaller rigs get up to speed quicker when entering an interstate highway.

If fulltiming is in your plans, an RV that's too small won't be satisfactory. Look for a unit in which you will be comfortable for long periods—one that allows you to go about the business of living (cooking, dining, bathing, relaxing, enjoying hobbies) without any inconvenience. It is more difficult to find a trailer for fulltiming than for any other use; it often requires much searching and shopping.

If you select a large unit, it will need some expensive options. In order to run the roof air conditioner of a motorhome while traveling, you'll need a generator; the dashboard air conditioner can't do the job. Most trailers and motorhomes more than 30 feet long need two air conditioners and perhaps two furnaces to adequately cool and heat the unit.

As trailer size increases, so must the pulling power of the tow vehicle; the purchase of a suitable truck may be required for towing a large trailer.

The larger the unit, the less economical it will be to operate. Large RVs weigh more than small RVs; consequently, they require large engines, which consume more fuel than small engines, to move them. The largest motorhomes are the worst fuel guzzlers; some average under 5 miles per gallon. Towing an auxiliary vehicle behind a motorhome further increases fuel consumption. It makes good sense not to drive or tow any more length and weight than necessary.

Because we are working fulltimers and need extra workspace and storage areas, we went from a 23-foot conventional trailer to a 29-foot fifth-wheel. With the larger size, however, came limitations: We can no longer stay in some of our favorite U.S. Forest Service campgrounds. We also must be more selective about our routes; we are pulling more weight, so we try to avoid long, steep grades. And, of course, we don't have the fuel economy we once had. We have adjusted to this trailer and its limitations, and, since it is big enough for our needs, we have no desire to move up to a larger size. We don't want to be more restricted in our traveling and camping than we are now.

A Comparison of Self-propelled and Towable RVs

Potential RV purchasers, especially those who haven't previously owned an RV, often have trouble deciding whether they want a self-propelled RV (a motorhome) or the type that must be towed (a trailer). Following are a few facts about the different types.

A motorhome costs more than a comparably sized trailer because, in addition to the living area, the price includes the same components— engine, drive train, and such—as any automobile or truck. The expense can sometimes be justified if the motorhome is small and easily maneuverable and can thus serve as a second car. If a tow vehicle must be purchased along with a trailer, in some instances the cost of the two units can approach that of a motorhome.

Unless an auxiliary vehicle is towed behind a motorhome, the motorhome itself has to be used for transportation once at your destination, making it necessary to break camp. A trailer's tow vehicle is not so encumbered; you can drive it away without disturbing the trailer and hookups. A tow vehicle, especially a truck, is suitable for exploring backcountry roads, whereas a typically low-slung motorhome is not.

Many motorhomers want to tow a small car to use once the motorhome is parked in a campsite. Even if you already own a suitable car, you have to purchase towing equipment. The simplest and least expensive equipment is a tow bar. With a tow bar, however, all four wheels are on the ground; some cars, according to manufacturers' recommendations, shouldn't be towed this way. A more costly tow dolly, which elevates the drive wheels of the car, may have to be used.

If you purchase a trailer, you'll also need the proper hitch equipment. Some dealers include this in the overall price of a small unit, but others do not. Be sure to have a hitch capable of pulling the weight of your trailer (Table 2-1). And you will need a tow vehicle with the power to pull the weight of the trailer. On trailers with electric brakes, a brake controller has to be installed in the tow vehicle.

If you decide against a trailer because of the hitching or backing involved and opt for a motorhome, you will be in the hitching business anyway if you want to tow a car. Moreover, backing only the motorhome is easy, but backing with a car attached ranges from difficult to impossible. Backing a trailer is much simpler.

Changing a flat tire on a mid-size or larger motorhome can be a problem. The average RVer has neither the physical strength nor the space to carry the equipment needed to change the large, heavy tires. Changing a flat, even on a large trailer, isn't much more difficult than changing a car or truck tire.

Although moving about in a motorhome under way may violate state seatbelt laws and is an unsafe practice that we do not recommend, this facet appeals to many people who like the options of using the toilet and preparing snacks and simple meals while rolling down the road. These conveniences sometimes influence their decision to purchase a motorhome rather than a trailer.

Table 2-1. Conventional Trailer Hitch Selection Guide

	Weight-Carrying Hitch			Weight-Distributing Hitch	
	Class I	Class II	Class III	Class III	Class IV
Trailer Weight:	2,000 lb.	3,500 lb.	5,000 lb.	4,000 lb.	10,000 lb.
Tongue Weight:	200 lb.	300 lb.	500 lb.	350 lb.	1,000 lb.
Vehicle type: Compact cars	Yes	No	No	No	No
Mid-size Cars	Yes	Yes	Yes	Yes	No
Full-size Cars	Yes	Yes	Yes	Yes	Yes
Mid-size Pickups/vans	Yes	Yes	Yes	Yes	Yes
Full-size Pickups/vans	Yes	Yes	Yes	Yes	Yes
Hitch Types	Receiver or step-bumper	Receiver or step-bumper	Receiver or step-bumper	Receiver only	Receiver only

Notes:

Many vehicles have manufacturer-imposed restrictions regarding towing requirements and may require additional equipment. Some vehicles may have the capability to tow more weight than this table suggests. Consult the manufacturers' literature for hitch information.

Use of step-bumper hitches on pickup trucks is limited to the manufacturers' weight restrictions.

Fifth-wheel hitches are rated by towing weight only; they have no classification.

Points About Different RV Types

Conventional and Fifth-Wheel Trailers

No matter which type of trailer you select, either conventional or fifth-wheel, you'll need a suitable tow vehicle equipped with the proper hitch

Figure 2-1. *A Jayco Jay Series conventional trailer.* *(Courtesy Jayco, Inc.)*

Figure 2-2. *This Skamper fifth-wheel trailer features a rear, curbside entry door. (Courtesy Skamper Corporation)*

to pull it (Figures 2-1 and 2-2). For towing the smallest, lightweight (under 2,000 pounds) conventional trailers, a small or mid-size car or truck with just a ball hitch on the rear bumper may suffice. Towing most conventional trailers, however, requires a substantial weight-distributing hitch, consisting of a hitch receiver, a draw-bar ball mount, spring bars for proper weight distribution, and a sway-bar control. Fifth-wheel trailers can be towed only by a pickup truck because the hitch must be mounted in the truck's bed.

Towing any type of trailer should be effortless and the sway from passing trucks and crosswinds minimal if the trailer is hitched correctly with the proper hitch equipment. Fifth-wheel trailers are less affected by passing trucks and strong winds than conventional trailers. As for maneuverability, the fifth-wheel offers the most flexibility. It can be backed more easily and turned in a tighter radius than a conventional trailer.

A fifth-wheel trailer of any given length generally has more storage space than a conventional trailer of the same length.

Motorhomes
Many RVers prefer a Class A or Class C motorhome because they don't have to go outside to reach the living quarters once it is parked (Figures

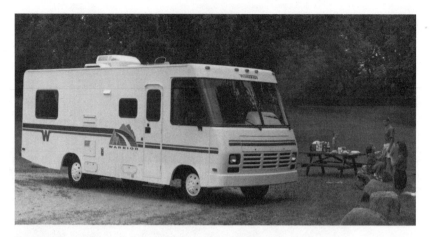

Figure 2-3. *A boxy but often aerodynamic shape identifies an RV as a Class A motorhome, such as this Warrior manufactured by Winnebago.*
(Courtesy Winnebago Industries, Inc.)

2-3 and 2-4). This is handy when it's raining; setting up camp can be put off until the rain stops.

In a Class A motorhome, the captain's chairs in the cockpit are designed to swivel around to become part of the living room. Some people, however, don't want to spend the evening relaxing in the same chair they were sitting in all day during travel. Some also prefer being in a different environment, such as a trailer affords, rather than being in the same unit day and night.

Another advantage of a motorhome is that if it's parked where suspicious activities are occurring, you can leave in a hurry without having to go outside.

Automotive repairs and routine maintenance are considerably more expensive for Class A motorhomes. The hourly labor rate is usually higher because what may be simple jobs on other vehicles are time-consuming and difficult on motorhomes. The larger the motorhome, the more its equipment costs; it's not at all unusual for a set of tires to cost more than $1,000.

Class C and micro-mini motorhomes are easily driven and maneuvered by anyone who can drive a car. They are very practical for boondocking, can be taken on rough roads, and are easily parked in just about any spot that takes your fancy. The height, low clearance, and long wheel base of some Class A models, however, make them imprac-

Figure 2-4. *This Jamboree Class C motorhome has the distinctive cabover bunk that identifies all Class C motorhomes.* (Courtesy Fleetwood Enterprises, Inc.)

tical for this type of traveling and camping.

Because smaller motorhomes are so versatile and have good fuel economy, it is often not necessary to tow a small car for local driving; this opens up the possibility for towing a boat trailer instead. If the motorhome will be used for towing a dinghy, determine whether or not a hitch can be installed at the rear of the motorhome.

Folding Tent Trailers

Folding tent trailers (Figure 2-5) are often considered the RV for beginners, but not everyone who chooses a tent trailer intends to move up

Figure 2-5. *This Starcraft model, like all folding tent trailers, collapses into a small, low-profile, easy-to-tow unit.* (Courtesy Starcraft RV, Inc.)

to a motorhome or hard-sided trailer in the future. The reason is that tent trailers can provide a unique camping experience because they have certain features not found on any other type of RV.

In no other RV can you live in an environment that encompasses so much of the outdoors. Even a tent does not provide such an outdoor experience. Most tents are windowless so, once you're inside, the outside world is completely closed off from view. To further enhance the outdoor experience, some tent trailers include a removable stove, sink, and dining table, which can be taken outside or used in a screened room—an option offered by most tent trailer manufacturers.

Other appealing features of tent trailers are their towability and storability. Their folded-down height is about 4 feet—lower than that of the most compact car—so there is little wind resistance while towing. Most tent trailers weigh less than 2,000 pounds—some are less than 1,000 pounds—so they can be towed by the smallest car. Whatever the tow vehicle, the low weight and minimal drag result in good fuel economy. A tent trailer can be stored in a standard size garage or kept in an out-of-the-way location in a yard. The front dolly wheel makes it easily maneuverable by hand.

Before purchasing a folding tent trailer, ask the salesperson to

Figure 2-6. *As its name implies, a pickup camper is mounted on a pickup truck. On pickup campers smaller than the Lance model shown, the rear is flush with the truck's tailgate. (Courtesy Lance Camper Manufacturing Corporation)*

Figure 2-7. *Skamper Corporation manufactures pickup campers with a pop-top.*
(Courtesy Skamper Corporation)

demonstrate the setting-up sequence. Note the time it takes—it should take about 10 to 15 minutes—and the complexity of the procedure. Then ask yourself if you want to perform this operation every time you arrive at a campsite, no matter how tired you are or what the weather.

Pickup Campers

Pickup campers are also versatile RVs (Figure 2-6). Models are available to fit all long- and short-bed trucks. The living area in this type of RV isn't as spacious as in some other RVs because it is limited by the size of the pickup truck's bed. Still, we have seen pickup campers that sleep six—in rather close quarters, however. Pickup campers have the same basic equipment as any small RV, except that some manufacturers do not include a toilet in the smallest units.

Increasingly popular are the pickup camper models with a roof that can be raised—a so-called pop-up or fold-down model (Figure 2-7). (This type of roof is also found on some small conventional trailers.) The roof is easily raised, usually with a crank mechanism, providing standing headroom inside. When the roof is dropped for traveling, the low profile of the camper causes little wind resistance, resulting in good fuel economy. The top-heavy feel that sometimes occurs when cornering with a hard-sided camper does not exist with pop-up models.

The box portion of a typical pickup camper that fits in the bed of a full-size pickup truck is about 8 feet long. Larger campers may have an additional 3 or 4 feet on the rear, extending beyond the truck's bed. The cabover portion, which contains a bed, may be 4 or 5 feet long.

When the truck is needed for other purposes, the pickup camper can be removed easily. Legs on each of the four corners of the camper box extend to the ground, and are then used to raise the camper enough to pull the truck out from under it (see Figure 2-6). After removing the truck, you can still use the camper as living quarters by lowering it on the legs to the point where it can be supported by concrete blocks or another type of sturdy support.

Camping Van Conversions

Of all RVs, camping van conversions have the least moving-around space. They are no wider than a standard van and may not have full standing headroom, but many have a number of amenities ingeniously crammed into the available space (Figure 2-8).

One advantage of a camping van conversion is that it can function as a second car because of its compact size and maneuverability. It can also be used as a tow vehicle for pulling a small trailer.

Figure 2-8. *A camping van conversion, such as the Falcon shown here, has a great deal of livability in a small space. The typically raised roof provides standing headroom.* (Courtesy International Vehicles Corporation)

Optional Equipment

The options needed or wanted depend on the RV and how it will be used. Fulltimers may want a great many options, while those who use an RV for vacations and occasional weekends may find the standard equipment sufficient for their needs. Some manufacturers offer few options because the standard equipment includes what other manufacturers offer as options. Some dealers order units with popular options or add them after arrival on their lots.

The three most popular options are an air conditioner, TV antenna, and microwave oven. Even if the RV isn't factory-equipped with these items, it is likely to be pre-wired so the dealer can install the equipment.

Many manufacturers build a galley cabinet just the right size to accommodate a microwave oven and install an electric receptacle for it. If a buyer opts for a microwave, it's a simple matter for the dealer to install it. You can install a microwave yourself, providing you can do it in such a way as to allow enough ventilation around the oven and anchor it securely. We installed our microwave—smaller than the optional one—because we didn't want to lose all the storage space in the cabinet.

Another popular option is an awning. Almost all RVs are factory-equipped with an awning rail so an awning can be easily added.

Some RVs have the options of factory-installed TVs and stereo equipment. Often a similar or the same TV can be purchased separately for less than the manufacturer's or dealer's option price. A built-in stereo in a motorhome may be an automotive type and provide a sound quality worth its cost; in trailers, however, this may not be the case. Only a few trailer manufacturers install quality name-brand stereos. If the stereo offered is a brand you've never heard of, it may be best to pass on this option. Again, you can probably purchase a quality unit for the same amount or less than the option price and have it independently installed or install it yourself. Radio reception on a portable stereo with an internal antenna isn't too good inside an RV because of the RV's metal skin. Any installed stereo or TV should be hooked up to an exterior antenna.

Slideout options are offered by many fifth-wheel trailer and some motorhome and conventional trailer manufacturers. The first slideouts, which were only on fifth-wheel trailers, contained either a living room sofa or a dinette. Later, two slideouts were offered: one for the sofa, the other for the dinette. On some units, this evolved into one long slideout that contained both the sofa and dinette. Next, some fifth-wheel manufacturers began offering a bedroom slideout; buyers now can opt for one, two, or three slideouts.

One or more slideouts may seem desirable, but after considering all the ramifications, this may not be a practical option. If you travel nearly every day during a vacation, with long days on the road, do you want to deal with the slideout each time you set up camp, or leave it unextended and put up with cramped conditions? Most slideouts are operated on the RV's 12-volt electrical system, with a provision for manual operation. It takes one or two minutes to extend a slideout using electric power, considerably longer if it is cranked out by hand. Slideout options may be more practical for those who travel to a destination and stay put for a period of days or weeks.

Another consideration is finding a campground where a slideout can be used. The sites in many older campgrounds are too narrow to accommodate RVs with slideouts extended.

The slideout option can increase the weight of the trailer by as much as 500 pounds or more for each slideout. (Other weight considerations are discussed later in this chapter.)

When it comes to choosing options, keep this in mind: One dealer said he never encountered any customers who were dissatisfied because they had too many. This being the case, why not have all the options you want if your budget allows?

Prices

Although purchase prices change every year, almost always moving higher, the relative prices of RV categories remain about the same. When comparing RV categories, there often isn't much price difference between the largest, most luxurious RV in one category and the smallest economy model in another. For example, some large trailers cost more than small motorhomes.

Generally, folding tent trailers are the least expensive and Class A motorhomes the most expensive, especially bus conversions. Folding tent trailers can be purchased for about $5,000; a super-deluxe bus conversion can cost a hundred times that amount and more.

Pickup campers fall into a slightly higher price range than folding tent trailers. Many conventional trailers are priced in the $10,000-to-$15,000 range, and even some fifth-wheel trailers can be purchased for about $15,000; however, on a foot-for-foot basis, a fifth-wheel of any given size costs more than a conventional trailer of the same size.

The majority of mid-size and large travel trailers range from $15,000 to a little more than $20,000; however, many are in the $30,000-to-$40,000 range and a few are priced as high as $70,000 to $80,000.

The smallest Class C motorhomes cost from $20,000 to $30,000; larger Class Cs are priced upward from $40,000. Prices for Class A motorhomes begin around $35,000.

The average price for most camping van conversions is about $33,000, but many units are priced higher or lower.

Prices stated here are very general and are only meant to provide a rough idea of what a certain type of RV may cost. Some units within each category cost less than the lowest price mentioned.

Options increase the cost of an RV by hundreds of dollars on small units and by thousands of dollars on large ones.

Used Units: Getting into RVing Inexpensively

The most economical way to get into RVing inexpensively is to purchase a used unit. The amount you spend can be a fraction of what a comparable new unit costs. Many units are for sale by owners who, for one reason or another, purchased the unit and then hardly used it; these are often very good buys.

An RV that is in good general condition but the interior is somewhat the worse for wear—worn upholstery, faded draperies, a soiled carpet—may be offered at a very low price. You can refurbish such an RV attractively without spending too much money. New window treatments, carpeting, and reupholstered or replaced furniture may be all it needs.

If you have a limited amount to spend, think small, especially if you are new to RVing. Purchasing a small unit gives you the opportunity to see if you really enjoy RVing without spending a great deal of money.

Small units weigh less than larger units, so less gasoline or diesel fuel is consumed. It also costs less to maintain a small RV. When replacing tires, single-axle trailers need only two tires instead of the four or six needed for multiple-axle trailers, and less expensive, smaller tires can be used. Fewer wheels also cut down the cost of routine wheel-bearing and brake maintenance.

Used, self-propelled RVs require more investigation prior to purchase than used towables. No matter how nice the living accommodations are in a used motorhome, the engine has seen some wear; in some respects, buying a used motorhome is no different than buying a used car.

When considering a used pickup camper, be aware that campers manufactured before 1988 and designed for use in full-size pickup trucks will fit into Ford and Dodge trucks, but not 1988 and later-model General Motors trucks. Although most full-size pickup campers manufactured after 1988 fit into all pickup truck beds, it is wise to check truck and camper compatibility before committing yourself.

Carefully inspect all areas of a used RV. Look for evidence of leaks inside (stains on the ceiling or walls) and outside. A build-up of caulking, or an amateurish job of calking—on roof seams especially—indicates a past leak; you may not be able to determine whether it has been fixed. If the RV has a musty wet-wood smell, dry rot—caused by water leaks—is probably present in wooden structural members or flooring. Be suspicious of a spongy feel to any floor areas. Check the floor around the base of the toilet for evidence of leaking.

Sight down the sides and ends of an RV to see that its lines are true. If not, it may have been in an accident that affected structural members, or the chassis may be warped from overloading. Don't forget to inspect the undercarriage. If the underbody is enclosed with metal or a flexible material, check for rips and cracks.

Ask the current owner or dealer to demonstrate how all appliances and equipment work.

The refrigerant used in the air-conditioning system of a tow vehicle, motorhome, or van conversion may be a consideration when buying used instead of new. The CFC refrigerant known as R-12, or Freon, which has been used almost universally in vehicle air-conditioning systems, will be outlawed in 1995. Until then, leaks in an air-conditioning system with this refrigerant can be repaired, but only authorized service technicians can purchase R-12, and its cost is soaring.

The replacement refrigerant, HFC-134a, is not compatible with R-12 and cannot be used to recharge a system that has had R-12 in it. If a leak develops in the air-conditioning system of some vehicles built during 1993, and all vehicles built before 1993, owners have two choices: Do without air conditioning or have the R-12 cleaned out and replaced with HFC-134a—a process that typically costs about $800.

No problem exists with refrigerant in roof air conditioners of used RVs; that won't be outlawed until 2015. RV refrigerators are the absorption type rather than the residential compressor type and don't use the problem refrigerants.

Weight Considerations

Those who have not purchased an RV before are often unaware of the importance of weight ratings. Indeed, even some experienced RVers pay little attention to this information, but certain calculations regarding weight should be made before purchasing any RV.

Weight information appears in most manufacturers' brochures, but sometimes it is omitted—probably because a unit doesn't stack up well in the weight department. Some weights are listed on a label on the exterior of trailers and on a doorpost on motorized RVs.

Dry weight is the weight of the unit without water, propane, and, in the case of motorhomes, engine fuel in the tanks. Wet weight, the weight of the unit with all tanks full (except holding tanks), is figured by multiplying the capacity of a tank by the weight of what is carried in it. The weights for a gallon of wet consumables are listed in Table 2-2. (The 6 or 10 gallons the water heater holds is not usually included in the manufacturer's wet-weight figure.)

Table 2-2. Weight of Liquid Consumables

Consumable	Pounds per Gallon
Propane	4.25
Gasoline	6.15
Diesel fuel	7.10
Water	8.30

Note:
   When calculating the wet weight for an RV with holding tanks full, use the weight for water for all holding-tank capacities.

The gross vehicle weight rating (GVWR) is the maximum amount the RV can safely carry. It includes the wet weight and the cargo weight—cargo being everything you want to load aboard your RV.

The cargo weight allowance is arrived at by subtracting the wet weight from the GVWR. When totaling the weights for cargo, the weights of all passengers who will ride in motorhomes and van conversions must be included. When calculating weight allowances for a pickup camper, the GVWR of the pickup truck is used. The weight of the camper is included with the wet consumables, including engine fuel, cargo, and passengers, and should not exceed the truck's GVWR.

Manufacturers, knowing that RVs will be loaded with food, clothing, recreational equipment, full water and propane tanks, and engine fuel (in motorhomes), should build units to safely carry all this without exceeding the GVWR. Some do, but some don't. The cargo-carrying capacity of some RVs is thousands of pounds, yet others can carry only *a few hundred pounds* before exceeding the GVWR. Just because two RVs are the same type and size, they won't necessarily have equal or even similar cargo-carrying capacity. Something else should not be taken for granted: A larger unit of one type of RV does not necessarily have more cargo-carrying capacity than a smaller unit of the same type.

We have even found some units with what—for lack of an official name—we have dubbed a "negative cargo-carrying capacity": The weight of the unit with the tanks filled exceeds the GVWR, leaving absolutely no allowance for any cargo. One 34-foot motorhome we checked was actually overloaded by almost 200 pounds with only the water, propane, and fuel tanks filled; another motorhome, 3½ feet shorter, with the tanks full was 4,000 pounds shy of the GVWR. It would take considerable cargo and quite a few heavyweight passengers to overload the smaller motorhome.

In another comparison of weight ratings between two conventional trailers, both the same length, one could carry twice the number of pounds of cargo than the other before being overloaded.

When calculating weight, any optional equipment of significant weight must be added to the dry weight of the RV (Table 2-3). Check the manufacturer's brochure to see whether equipment is listed as standard or optional. All standard equipment is normally included in the manufacturer's dry-weight figure.

Those who want to tow an auxiliary vehicle or boat behind a

motorhome should be concerned with the gross combined vehicle weight rating (GCVWR). The wet weight of the motorhome, the weights of cargo and passengers, and the weight of the towed item should not exceed the GCVWR.

Trailerists must consider the GCVWR of the tow vehicle, which should not be exceeded after adding the wet weight of the trailer, cargo in both the trailer and tow vehicle (including engine fuel), and the passengers' weights.

With fifth-wheel trailers, the payload rating, or cargo-carrying capacity, of the truck must be higher than the hitch weight of the trailer, plus the weight of the hitch, passengers, and any equipment and fuel carried in the truck. (A fiver's hitch weight must be considered as payload since the hitch is in the truck's bed.)

The hitch, or tongue, weight of a conventional trailer should be no less than 11 percent of the loaded trailer's weight (a too-light hitch weight will adversely affect handling while towing) and must not exceed the recommended weight rating for the class of hitch used (see Chapter 6 for more about hitch weight).

RV shoppers should check the weight ratings and do some simple calculations to determine the cargo-carrying capacity of a unit, and then also estimate the weight of the cargo. This cannot be determined with a great deal of accuracy so, to be on the safe side, always overestimate the cargo weight.

A safety factor is built into all weight ratings, but overloading should be avoided for several reasons:

Table 2–3. Typical Weights of Optional RV Equipment

Equipment	Weight in Pounds
Air conditioner	100
Awning	80–135
Generator	100–250
Automatic levelers	250
TV	30
Microwave oven	50–75
Slideout	500–1,500

• Driving or towing an overloaded RV is dangerous.

• Overloading can void warranties.

• Continually overloading an RV shortens its longevity.

• Keeping weight down aids in fuel conservation; every hundred pounds added increases fuel consumption by about 2 percent.

• Less weight means less wear on the engine and other moving parts.

• The less weight tires carry, the longer they last.

Shopping Tips

Once you have made the major decision to purchase a trailer or motorhome and have figured out the approximate size you need, an important decision remains: Which RV, of all the many brands and models of the type and size you want, is the one for you?

Trying to choose from the seemingly endless array of different manufacturers' models, floorplans, prices, standard and optional features, and decor can be confusing. Some shoppers wearily, and often unwisely, decide to purchase an RV because they simply cannot face trekking through yet another unit.

Be aware at the outset that there is little chance of finding an RV that is absolutely perfect for you in all respects; compromises have to be made. Before you begin serious shopping, make a detailed list of everything you want and need. So nothing is overlooked, include obvious things such as the number of beds required. If you need storage space for recreational equipment, such as fishing rods or golf bags, add it to the list. Items to check, such as capacity of holding tanks, battery space, and space for a microwave oven, should also be on the list.

When you arrive at a dealer's lot, first pick up the brochures for the RVs that interest you. Then, as you inspect each one, jot down its pros and cons on the brochure. A notebook for extra comments is helpful. Back home, it will be easier to remember individual units if you have a written record of your impressions.

It may take several visits to different dealers to narrow down your top-rated units to one or two. At this point, make as many visits to the dealer as necessary. Keep a running list of questions about the unit under consideration, then quiz the salesperson each time you visit. Don't worry about making a nuisance of yourself; you have every right to take as much time as you need—it's your money at stake.

When we were shopping for our present trailer, it took four months and many visits to different towns to find one suitable for our lifestyle. Because we are working fulltimers, we had to find an RV that could function as both a comfortable home and an efficient office.

When we first saw the trailer we later purchased, we dismissed it as not right for us. As we continued to look at other units, however, it began to look better. During many visits to the dealer, we measured every storage space, tried out all the equipment, picked the salesperson's brain, and even made several calls to the factory to find out if certain modifications could be made. We finally decided on the trailer that had seemed unsuitable at the beginning.

Where to Shop

For those who have never owned an RV, the best place to do preliminary shopping is at RV shows. All types of RVs are on display and you can wander through all of them to your heart's content, or until your legs give out. Realistically, hardly anyone has the stamina to look at all RVs displayed unless it's a very small show. Serious shoppers limit themselves to the type of RV they want within their price range.

Don't be pressured into buying any RV you have doubts about even though the so-called "show price" is attractive. Chances are, you can get the same price once the unit is back on the dealer's lot.

RV shows are advertised in local newspapers and often on TV. It may be worth your while to visit shows that are some distance from your immediate locality.

If you can't get to any shows, or none are held in your vicinity, make the rounds of dealers. Again, don't hesitate to go afield to visit dealers; each dealer carries only a few brands of RVs. You will be spending thousands of dollars, so spending time to find out what's available is sensible.

Other shopping aids are the *Trailer Life and MotorHome RV Buyer's Guide* and *Woodall's RV Buyer's Guide*. Both list hundreds of units, covering a wide representation of RV types. Each listing includes a photograph of the unit, floorplan, statistics (height, length, weight, cargo allowance, and tank capacities), construction method and materials, standard equipment, furnace and air-conditioning specifications, and approximate price.

Both guides are published annually and can be found on newsstands in the spring, or they can be ordered from the publishers: Woodall Publishing Company, 1-800-323-9076; and TL Enterprises, 1-800-234-3450. Each issue of *Trailer Life* and *MotorHome* features at least one in-depth review of an RV, as well as other articles of interest to RVers. The monthly magazines can be found on newsstands; for subscription information, call 1-800-678-1201.

Financing

No matter how tight credit is or how difficult it is to obtain loans for automobiles and houses, anyone with a good credit history usually encounters no problems in financing the purchase of an RV. RV buyers have proven to be good credit risks; their loan delinquency rate is very low and repossessions are less than 1 percent.

Since an RV holds much of its value during the term of the loan— they don't depreciate as quickly as cars—many RV loans can be repaid over a period of up to 10 years; the term for a new, expensive RV can be 15 years.

The down payment required is usually 20 percent of the total cost, but it can be as low as 10 percent. Depending on the lender, credit life insurance, disability insurance, taxes, licensing fees, extra accessories, and an extended warranty can be included in the loan. A financed RV must be adequately covered by insurance.

RVs can be financed by the same lending institutions that provide house mortgages and automobile loans: banks, savings and loan associations, credit unions, and finance companies. Dealers often put together attractive loan packages—doing the paperwork, arranging for insurance in some cases—so you can purchase the unit quickly without shopping around for the best loan. Dealer-arranged financing, called indirect financing, is so convenient that such RV purchases far outnumber those made through direct financing, where the buyer arranges for the loan. Because dealers generally work through one or more local lending institutions, they can sometimes offer lower interest rates than those direct financing offers.

If the dealer sells a certain brand of RV, the loan may be arranged through the manufacturer. RV manufacturers have recognized that loans are a profitable adjunct to their businesses, as General Motors and Ford discovered years ago when they set up financing entities for their automobiles.

Before signing on the dotted line, consider the total cost of the RV and other costs included in the loan package, down-payment requirements, length of the loan, and how comfortable the repayment plan. As with any loan, read all the fine print on all documents. If you intend to pay off the loan before its term has expired, the contract should provide for prepayment without penalties.

For first-time RV buyers, a short-term loan and a large down payment may be best. After gaining some experience, it's not unusual for newcomers to decide they want a different size or type of RV.

If you have been putting off purchasing an RV because you don't want to finance it, consider this: The recently revised tax laws eliminated all interest deductions except for first and second homes. An RV with galley, sleeping quarters, and bath falls into the second-home category. As long as you don't have another second home and the RV is the collateral on the loan, the interest can be taken as a deduction on your federal income taxes.

Extended Warranties

Although most products are automatically covered by a manufacturer's warranty that runs for a period of months to several years, extended warranties are routinely offered and sold to buyers. The new RV owner has the opportunity to purchase extended warranties for some of the major appliances and equipment, such as the air conditioner, refrigerator, generator, and furnace. Extended warranties are offered in addition to service contracts that cover automotive functions on motorhomes and vans.

Are extended warranties worth the money? Usually not, no matter what they cost. According to the Service Contract Industry Council, 80 percent of all extended warranties are never used. Most inherent problems in today's products, especially those with electronics, occur within three to six months of purchase, when the item is still covered by the initial manufacturer's warranty. The initial warranty reduces the value of nearly all extended warranties. For example: If the initial warranty is good for one year and the extended warranty is good for three years, in effect, you are receiving only two years of extended warranty coverage.

Not all extended warranties must be purchased with the RV, but there is a time limit—usually a few weeks—after which the extended warranty cannot be purchased. Be sure you know what an extended warranty covers. In many cases, it is worded the same as the initial warranty, except for the period of coverage; in some cases, the wording is ambiguous. Some warranties contain a sentence similar to this: "This warranty covers only specified parts (or components)." Find out exactly which parts or components are covered. Although some manufacturers use the word "parts," don't be surprised if the warranty applies to one part. "Parts" may refer to only the compressor of the air conditioner, or the cooling unit of the refrigerator, or the combustion chamber of the furnace.

All warranties should always be kept somewhere in the RV—it won't do you any good if you have a problem on the road and the warranty is at home. We keep all warranties and operating manuals together in a large envelope so we have only one place to look when we need these documents.

Service Contracts

A service contract is often offered to motorhome and van conversion buyers, the initial cost of which can range from several hundred to more than a thousand dollars. There also may be a deductible for every repair. If the vehicle is sold or the service contract is canceled, transfer and cancellation fees may be involved.

Buyers should be aware of exactly what the service contract covers. It should not duplicate the warranty provisions. If the vehicle has a good warranty, a service contract purchase sometimes can be delayed until the original warranty runs out.

Understand who will back the service contract. It may be the manufacturer or the dealer, or it may be turned over to an independent company, called an administrator. If any of these go out of business, who will handle the contract? Is this spelled out in the contract? Is the backer insured (required in some states) by a reputable company? Check with your state's consumer protection office and Better Business Bureau to determine whether complaints have been filed against the backers. The solvency and reliability of insurance companies can be obtained from the state insurance commission.

It is especially important for RVers to pay particular attention to the requirements for repairs. Since motorhomes and van conversions are usually purchased for travel, the contract should allow repairs to be done at service centers other than in the area where the RV was purchased. Some companies allow service only in a specific geographical area.

Read the contract carefully to determine what is covered. If a certain repair is not listed, assume it is not covered. Be alert for clauses that deny coverage for any reason. A clause found in many contracts denies coverage if a covered part is damaged by a noncovered part. Another clause states that only mechanical breakdowns are covered, thus eliminating normal wear-and-tear problems.

Terminology can affect whether a claim is denied. If the part in question is called by a name other than what the contract lists as a covered part, the claim may not be paid. If the engine is disassembled to diagnose the problem and noncovered parts are found to be the cause, the contract holder most likely will have to pay for the entire repair. The backer may not pay the entire cost of repairing or replacing a covered part if a depreciation factor is applied: The greater the number of miles, the less coverage.

If a motorhome or van is not regularly serviced for routine maintenance (keep all receipts), a claim may be denied or the contract voided. Obviously, service contract interpretation can be quite ambiguous.

Claim denial often occurs because the contract holder doesn't follow the prescribed method for obtaining repairs. Many contract holders must have authorization from the backer before any repairs are done or even a towing service used. We have heard of instances in which contract holders were forced to stay in motels and rent cars—at their own expense—because they were unable to reach the service contract backer for quick authorization.

Read the contract to find out how payments for covered repairs are handled. It may be your responsibility to pay for each repair, with later reimbursement only when the repair is deemed covered.

Insurance

Financed RVs must be insured, and RVs with engines must have the automotive insurance required by the state in which the RV is registered. Homeowner's insurance may adequately cover an RV if it is small and moderately priced and used only on weekends or short vacations. The provisions for RVs in homeowner's insurance policies, however, are often not adequate to cover RVing needs.

Carefully check the coverage for your RV in your homeowner's policy. Quiz your agent or the insurance company directly about any gray areas, including extended vacations, liability, and personal property. Coverage should be specifically spelled out in the policy; otherwise, claims may be disputed.

You may be covered when you use your RV for vacations, but will your insurer consider a trip of a month or more a vacation? Will you be covered if you live six months in your house, then take your RV to another location and live six months there?

Questions about liability coverage often arise when the RV is parked in a campsite as opposed to being towed or driven. Would you be covered if, say, someone tripped on your doormat and was injured? Or, as in an actual case we know of, if your propane tank exploded and neighboring RVers were injured by flying debris?

In many policies, personal property coverage is a token amount that would not begin to cover what you pack into an RV for a trip of any length. At extra cost, endorsements can be obtained to increase personal property coverage.

When shopping for RV insurance, be sure the company insures your type of RV. Make sure the agent understands exactly what type it is; too many think RVs are only motorhomes. Tell the agent how you will use your RV: weekends, short vacations, or extended usage. Know what coverage you want and need; then compare the coverage and rates of several companies (they vary considerably).

Tow Vehicles

If the RV you select is a trailer, you'll need a tow vehicle to pull it; the type you will need depends largely on the weight of the trailer. If the trailer is small and lightweight, you may already own a suitable tow vehicle: Many full-size and some compact passenger cars, sport utility vehicles, and vans can pull small trailers. The only class of vehicles that usually can't be used for towing are subcompact imports. You may even approach the purchase of a trailer by first investigating what your vehicle is capable of towing, and then shopping for a trailer with a suitable weight.

With an existing vehicle, check with the dealer for towing information. If a new vehicle will be part of your RVing package, visit the dealer first and pick up the manufacturer's towing guide; some include helpful towing tips (Ford has an excellent towing guide). If a towing guide is not offered by the manufacturer, the brochure for the vehicle you are considering should contain the necessary information.

Vehicles may need certain factory-installed equipment to be suitable for towing, so you may not be able to purchase what you need off the dealer's lot; however, because pickup trucks are so popular as tow vehicles, dealers often have models available with the factory-installed towing package.

Among other features, a towing package may contain an oversized radiator, heavy springs, transmission oil cooler, wiring harness, extended mirrors, and handling package. These items can be added to an existing vehicle, but it's usually less expensive to have the package installed at the factory. If a vehicle is used for towing and doesn't have the manufacturer's recommended equipment, the warranty can be voided.

When adding towing equipment to a vehicle, replace the turn-signal relay with a heavy-duty model because it will have to carry the additional load of the trailer turn signals. The relay is usually located in the fuse panel; replacing it is as simple as replacing a fuse.

Two important considerations for a tow vehicle are its engine and rear-axle ratio. Engine power pulls the load; for engine longevity, it should pull the load with as little effort as possible. For those with a moderately heavy trailer to tow, it is usually best to select the largest gasoline engine available. This is especially true if you plan to do considerable towing in mountainous areas. A diesel engine is excellent for heavy-duty towing. Although expensive to buy, it gets almost twice as many miles per gallon as a gasoline engine.

As for the rear-axle ratio, the heavier the load to be towed, the higher (numerically) the ratio should be. For example, an axle with a 4.10:1 ratio provides more pulling power than one with a 3.73:1 ratio and, incidentally, also causes the vehicle to burn proportionately more fuel. The vehicle you select should be factory-equipped with the needed rear-axle ratio; the towing guide provides this information. The dealer can change a rear-axle ratio, but the job can cost close to $1,000. Installed at the factory, the rear-axle option is about $50.

Automatic transmissions are usually recommended for towing and are generally rated to tow heavier loads than manual transmissions. If a tow vehicle has an overdrive transmission, most manufacturers recommend that the overdrive mode not be used when towing.

When selecting the model of a particular truck, be aware that towing weight ratings differ between regular-cab, super-cab, and crew-cab models. The super- and crew-cab vehicles are heavier than regular-cab models; consequently, their tow ratings are lower.

Whether a vehicle has two- or four-wheel drive also affects the weight it can pull. A vehicle with two-wheel drive is usually rated to tow several hundred pounds more than the same vehicle with four-wheel drive.

It may be assumed that a 1-ton truck would provide better towing capability than a ¾-ton truck, but this is not necessarily true. For example, the highest rear-axle ratio offered by Ford in any light pickup is 4.10:1. It wouldn't make much sense to spend extra money for a 1-ton truck if you only get stiffer springs (with the resultant rougher ride) and a heavyweight vehicle that consumes more fuel but has no additional towing capability.

When buying a tow vehicle, as with an RV, you will be spending thousands of dollars, so don't leave it up to salespeople to tell you what vehicle you should have. Often they don't know. They are interested in selling vehicles, and too many are inclined to assure you that what they are pushing will do the job. It's up to you to do the research to inform yourself so your money will be well spent.

A Truck for a Pickup Camper

Follow manufacturers' recommendations when selecting a truck for a pickup camper. Almost all truck styles, drives, and engines from all full-size truck manufacturers are suitable for use with pickup campers, but all manufacturers require that the truck be equipped with the camper package, which has many of the components of the towing package.

The largest pickup campers may need a 1-ton pickup truck because of its heavy-duty springs.

Along with the GVWR, the center of gravity (the balance point of the camper along a fore-and-aft axis measured in inches) must be considered so the truck won't have too much weight aft. Center-of-gravity information is in the camper manufacturer's brochure and on the Truck Consumer Information Sheet included with the documents owners receive.

Towing an Auxiliary Vehicle

It may be convenient to have an auxiliary vehicle available for sightseeing and errands instead of using the motorhome, but towing a dinghy is not without problems. Consult the owner's manual for the car to see if the manufacturer allows towing; some do not. The manufacturer may have certain towing requirements that must be adhered to so as not to void the warranty. If towing is approved, certain restrictions may apply about the distance and speed at which the car can be towed. If the owner's manual is used as the authority and the proper towing procedures are followed, the warranty should be honored if problems arise.

Some cars can be towed on all four wheels; others have to be towed with the drive wheels off the ground. When all four wheels are on the ground, a tow bar is used (Figure 2-9). Drive wheels are elevated on a tow dolly (Figure 2-10). If a manufacturer does not allow towing either way, a dinghy can be carried on its own flat-bed trailer.

The least expensive and simplest to use towing apparatus is a tow bar; however, additional equipment may be needed, such as a device to disconnect the car's drive shaft, an axle lock, or a pump to lubricate the car's transmission. Tow-dolly equipment varies according to the manufac-

Figure 2-9. *Using a tow bar is one method of towing an auxiliary vehicle behind a motorhome.*

(Courtesy Automatic Equipment Manufacturing Company)

Figure 2-10. *With a tow dolly, the drive wheels of an auxiliary vehicle are elevated for towing.* (Courtesy Automatic Equipment Manufacturing Company)

turer; some may offer brakes, a loading winch, a spare tire, and a suction-cup bar with tail, brake, and signal lights as options.

All of these towing methods require hitching and unhitching, so RVers who opt for a motorhome instead of a trailer to avoid this should not tow a dinghy. Additionally, when a tow dolly or flat-bed trailer is used, the car must be secured with chains or webbing tie-downs so it won't roll off.

Regulations concerning the licensing and titling of tow dollies vary from state to state, and some department of motor vehicle clerks may not be clear on the subject.

Another problem with dinghy towing includes braking. Conventional and fifth-wheel trailers are equipped with their own brakes; when the tow vehicle is braked, the trailer brakes are activated. When a tow bar is used to tow a car on all four of its wheels, the motorhome's brakes alone will have to stop or slow the motorhome plus the ton or more the dinghy weighs.

The weight of the towed vehicle and its towing equipment, plus the loaded weight of the motorhome, should not exceed the gross combined vehicle weight rating (GCVWR) of the motorhome. The frame or bumper of a motorhome may have to be reinforced before any towing can be done. A standard or optional hitch receiver is available on some motorhomes.

Thorough research is necessary to find a suitable auxiliary vehicle and the proper equipment with which to tow it.

Try a Rental Unit Before Buying

Renting before purchasing is a sensible idea if you have never owned an RV or had any RVing experience. Motorhomes of all types and sizes can be rented, but only small trailers are available.

Rental companies are located throughout the United States and Canada. Cruise America (1-800-327-7778) is the largest, with many offices in North America, and a large fleet of rental units. Local rental companies are listed in the Yellow Pages under "Recreational Vehicles, Renting and Leasing." Some companies offer one-way rentals—pick up the RV in one place and return it to another—as well as fly/drive options.

Where you intend to travel should influence the type of RV you rent. A large motorhome, for example, is not practical for visiting big cities. Aside from the difficulty of maneuvering in traffic, finding a place to park may be impossible.

Chapter 3

The Interior of an RV

A fter deciding on the type of RV you want, you'll have to choose an interior that meets your needs, including enough sleeping and eating accommodations, adequate bath facilities, and storage space for everyone who will use the RV regularly.

Floorplans

Manufacturers offer a variety of floorplans but are limited by the type of units they make. In a Class A motorhome, the living room is necessarily in the front because the cockpit chairs are designed to swivel toward the living room when the motorhome is parked. Beds are always positioned in the end fold-out sections in a folding tent trailer and in the cabover portion of pickup campers. A cabover bed is typical in Class C motorhomes, but the cabover section may contain cabinets when there is a rear bedroom.

Baths in RVs may be in the rear or the middle on one side or the other, or a mid-bath may be arranged with the facilities divided between both sides. Bedrooms in conventional trailers may be in the front or rear; they are almost always in the rear in Class A motorhomes and in

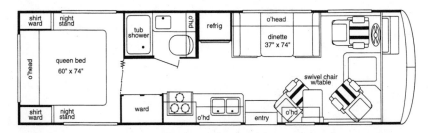

Figure 3-1. *A common Class A motorhome floorplan. (Courtesy Fleetwood Enterprises, Inc.)*

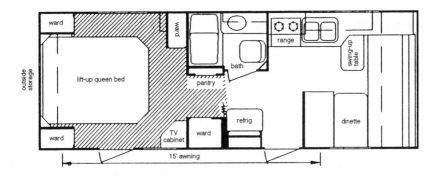

Figure 3-2. *This small conventional trailer features a front living room; other conventional trailers may have the galley or bedroom in the front.*
(Courtesy Skyline Corporation)

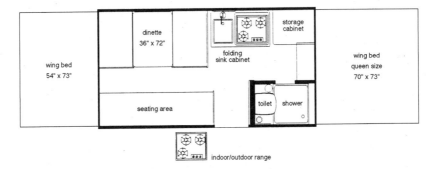

Figure 3-3. *A feature of any folding tent trailer is the roomy beds on each end. Depending on its size, a folding tent trailer may or may not have a bath.*
(Courtesy Skamper Corporation)

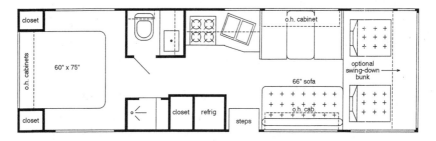

Figure 3-4. *A Class C motorhome floorplan may include a cabover bunk or, in some models, the cabover space may be devoted to storage.* *(Courtesy Tiffin Motorhomes, Inc.)*

the front in fifth-wheel trailers. For a couple of years, however, some fifth-wheel manufacturers put the living room in the front and the

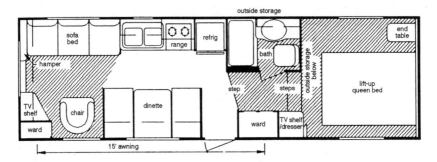

Figure 3-5. *Most fifth-wheel trailers feature a front bedroom with either the gal-ley or living room in the rear.* (Courtesy Skyline Corporation)

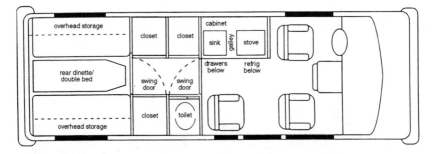

Figure 3-6. *Ingenuity figures in many camping van conversion floorplans. Here, the roomy dinette converts into a large bed.* (Courtesy Coach House, Inc.)

bedroom in the rear. Conventional trailer galleys and living rooms may be either in the front, rear, or middle. (Figures 3-1 through 3-7 illustrate common RV floorplans.)

Decor

Nearly all RVs have attractive, color-coordinated interiors that, in dis-play models, may be further enhanced by an artfully placed floral arrangement or basket of fruit and the dining table set for a cozy candle-light dinner. It would be the rare new or late model RV that did not create a pleasing impression upon entering. RV shoppers should not overlook this first impression, but they should not allow it to over-whelm them either. There's much more to consider when purchasing an RV than its interior appearance.

Unless you find the exact RV you want on the dealer's lot, you can order from the factory. This gives you the option of selecting the interior colors and fabrics. If small children will be staying in the RV, or if you want to cut down on housekeeping chores, choosing dark fabrics and carpeting rather than light ones may be more practical.

Folding tent trailers, pickup campers, and some small trailers may have vinyl floor covering throughout. Larger trailers have carpeting in all rooms except the galley, where vinyl floor covering or parquet is used.

Sleeping Accommodations

A primary consideration when purchasing an RV is that it have enough beds so all occupants will have a comfortable place to sleep. Even the smallest units, whether pickup campers, motorhomes, or trailers, generally have satisfactory sleeping accommodations for two adults and two children, although the beds may not be conventional. A sofa may convert into a standard double bed, a dinette may convert into a smaller double suitable for two children, and a large single bed may be formed by unfolding an overhead bunk. Large motorhomes and trailers usually have one double or queen-size conventional bed, or twin beds, as well as a convertible dinette and a sofa bed. Some trailer manufacturers make units ideal for families with a bedroom in the front, a

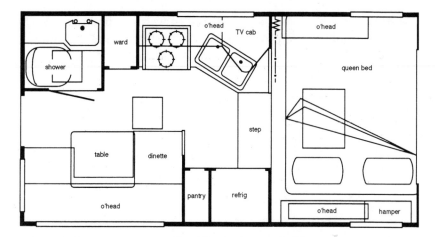

Figure 3-7. *Manufacturers of pickup campers cleverly get maximum livability from a small space. The 9-foot, 7-inch pickup camper shown here has sleeping accommodations for four, a bath with a shower, and a full galley.*
(*Courtesy Fleetwood Enterprises, Inc.*)

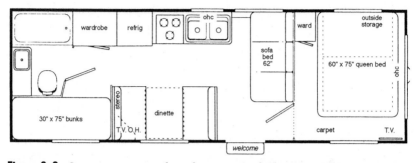

Figure 3-8. *Some conventional trailers are two-bedroom models with a front bedroom and two bunks in the rear. Both bedrooms can be closed off for privacy.* (Courtesy Kit Manufacturing Company)

convertible sofa or dinette (or both) in the middle, and two bunk beds in the rear (Figure 3-8).

When considering the purchase of a Class C or a micro-mini motorhome, think about who will sleep in the cabover berth. Climbing into the berth using the access ladder poses no problem for children, but tall adults, the elderly, and the infirm may find it inconvenient. Be aware that some cabover berths are not for the claustrophobic, no matter what their age.

Sleeping accommodations in folding tent trailers consist of two large beds, usually one queen size and one double, that fold out from the front and rear of the trailer. Often a convertible dinette or gaucho (a seat that pulls out or unfolds into a double bed) is included.

In some van conversions, the dining table and its seats, or a sofa,

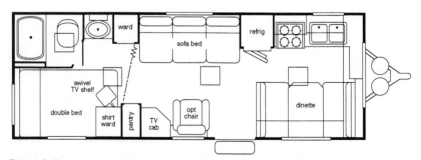

Figure 3-9. *In a small trailer, there is room for both a sofa and a dinette if the bath is located next to the bed. In most units with such floorplans, the lavatory is outside the enclosed compartment containing the toilet and shower.* (Courtesy Fleetwood Enterprises, Inc.)

may convert into a double bed. Some large van conversion models have two passenger seats that convert into single beds; if the model also has a convertible double bed, there are sleeping accommodations for four.

In order to have room for both a sofa and a dinette, some trailers in the 18- to 24-foot size have a fore-and-aft-facing bed in a rear corner, with a toilet/shower compartment right next to it (Figure 3-9). These beds are designated doubles, but they may be only 48 inches wide rather than the 54-inch standard double.

Enough beds of some type to sleep four or six are common in most RVs, except for the very smallest units; many RVs can sleep seven or eight. If the RV you want doesn't have enough sleeping accommodations for your family, perhaps children can sleep in a tent or in the bed of a pickup truck, if it is covered by a cap.

The Galley

Except for some folding tent trailers, pickup campers, and van conversions, most trailers and motorhomes have a well-equipped galley with a three- or four-burner range, an oven and ventilating hood, a refrigerator with a freezer, a double sink, and sufficient drawer and cabinet storage. A slideout pantry is a feature in some galleys.

What all too many RV galleys don't have is adequate counter space—some actually have less than 6 inches. Often a sink cover is provided (it may be optional) to increase counter space, but it is a poor substitute for real counter space and usually has to be stood on the floor or put in some other inconvenient place when you're using the sink. If a dining table is opposite the galley, it can double as a work area. Note whether the counter space in the RV you are considering is adequate for the type of cooking you do.

A galley located in the front or rear of a trailer is the most spacious and usually has ample counter space. Since their introduction, rear galleys have been very popular, but we wouldn't want the galley there for several reasons. The main problem is weight distribution; in a rear galley, much of the heavy equipment—refrigerator, range, microwave oven—ends up behind instead of over the axles, as is the case with a mid-galley, so all the weight is supported only by the chassis. Moreover, when a trailer is moving, more bounce is in the rear than in any other location, so there is a greater chance of dishes breaking and stored food spilling. Before traveling, special care must be taken to secure galley items to prevent damage.

Another reason we aren't in favor of either a rear or front galley is that with this positioning, the living room is in the middle, where there is the least ventilation and generally the worst view: The predominant scenery from a middle window is usually the RV parked in the next site. The living room is where we and, we suspect, other RVers spend the most time in daylight and evening hours. We prefer it to be in the prime location, which we consider to be the rear.

The Living Room and Dining Area

In very small RVs, there is no living room *per se* and a dinette provides the only seating. As RVs increase in size, more traditional living room furniture appears. In addition to a dinette, some units may have a sofa; others may have a sofa and a chair or two, one or both of which may be recliners, but slightly smaller than residential pieces. Perhaps there is a cabinet or table for holding a TV, and maybe a foldup table in addition to a dinette. Some large fifth-wheel trailers have a floor-to-ceiling hutch, part of which is devoted to an entertainment center—TV, VCR, stereo—and the rest to general storage.

It used to be that dining accommodations in RVs were always dinettes, but lately the trend among some manufacturers is to use a free-standing table and chairs. While attractive, this furniture eliminates the considerable storage space under a dinette's seats.

RV dinettes aren't often overly spacious. Many seat four average-size adults, but some have room for only two adults to sit comfortably. (A convertible dinette of this size would convert into a proportionately sized bed.)

The Bath

The size of the bath is governed by the size of the RV. Many van conversions and folding tent trailers do not have a bath at all, but some have a compartment for a portable toilet with a curtain or folding panel for privacy; others have an enclosed compartment containing a toilet and shower.

In small RVs, pickup campers especially, the enclosed compartment with the toilet doubles as the shower stall. The shower drain is in the center of the floor of the compartment. A tiny lavatory is molded into the fiberglass walls of the compartment and the shower hose is connected to its faucets. There may be a couple of molded-in storage cabinets.

In addition to a toilet, lavatory, and storage space, standard equipment in larger RVs includes a shower, which may be a stall or incorporated into a tub. Most stalls or tubs are smaller than those used in residences, but many are perfectly adequate for a satisfying shower or bath. A luxurious, full-size, glass-enclosed shower is a feature in some large fifth-wheel trailers and Class A motorhomes.

If the RV's bath is too small, or there are too many people who have to use it, campground showers and toilets can be used. All private campgrounds have these facilities, as do some state parks and other public parks. The facilities in a primitive campground, if any, are probably pit toilets.

Towel rods are often in short supply, so if more than two people occupy the RV, there may not be enough places to hang towels. Extra rods or hooks can sometimes be installed on the underside of the medicine chest, or on a wall, cabinet front, or bath door.

Storage Space

One of the most important factors in RV selection is adequate storage space for all occupants. Storage space should be cabinets or drawers, not open shelves. Anything stored on open shelves is likely to fall off when the RV is moving. Only clothes, linens, and other unbreakable items can be stored safely on open shelves.

If an RV is short on space for hanging clothes, some clothes normally hung on hangers can be folded or rolled and stored in drawers and cabinets.

Never assume there is storage space behind all cabinet doors. Open them to check it out—the area may contain the fuse panel, heating ducts, or plumbing lines, or it may be otherwise impractical storage. Check outside storage compartments, too. Nowadays many RVs have storage space under the bed, accessed by lifting the foot of the bed. In some RVs most of this area is taken up by the water tank.

Some manufacturers utilize space for storage better than others and include built-in storage units wherever possible, but shoppers will find many units in which space exists where cabinets can be installed. Even with space available, however, extra cabinets are rarely offered as options except on large, expensive RVs. Buyers of other types of RVs have to accept a unit as it comes from the factory.

Basement model RVs have huge compartments that are accessed from the outside. One or more of these cavernous areas may run across the full width of the RV, with an access door on each side. We've seen some compartments large enough to hold two full-size bicycles, with room to spare.

Those contemplating a basement model should realize that, in some units, filling up all the compartments with cargo can push the weight far above the GVWR. So, although the space may be there, you may not be able to utilize it fully.

Windows

When searching for an RV, many shoppers give little thought to the number of windows a unit has and whether they open. So many other important features figure into the selection of an RV that windows are often ignored, but they should be given due consideration.

There are times when an air conditioner can't be used—when camping without an electric hookup and you either don't have a generator or don't want to put up with generator noise. On mild days, when it's not warm enough to warrant using the air conditioner, you want to be able to open some windows to cool the unit. If RVing appeals to you because you like fresh air and the outdoors, look for a unit with enough windows to experience these pleasures.

Folding tent trailers have large zip-open windows on all four sides; ventilation is superior to that of any other type of RV. Among hard-sided RVs, trailers (especially conventional trailers) generally have more opening windows than motorhomes. The windshield and most rear windows on a motorhome cannot be opened.

We like windows for reasons other than ventilation. With lots of windows, an RV's interior is light and airy looking, not gloomy and dim. Windows are picture frames for the outdoors, and we enjoy looking at the ever-changing vistas.

On all RVs except folding tent trailers, opening windows are usually either the sliding or louvered type; in a few units the windows are opened by pushing out the bottom. Not all opening windows are suitable for providing ventilation. Sliding windows, for example, allow for only half the area to be open, and they can't be left open in the rain. With louvered windows, most of the area opens, so lots of fresh air and breezes can enter, and they can be left open in light to moderate rain. Bottom-opening windows won't allow rain to enter, but they don't open far enough to admit much fresh air either.

Window Coverings

The primary purpose of RV window coverings—whether draperies, blinds, or shades—is to provide privacy, and secondarily, to darken the room for sleep or to block sunlight. Certain window coverings can also aid in climate control and affect the amount of time spent housecleaning. All RVs come with some type of window covering as standard equipment, but the buyer may be able to select optional blinds or shades.

Older RVs often had nothing but draperies or curtains on the windows; mini-blinds, pleated shades, and roll-up window shades are now either standard or optional equipment.

Lined or heavy draperies alone can keep out the sun and light and provide privacy. A lining or backing of insulating material keeps out heat from the sun and some of the cold air transmitted from the window.

Window shades can be good heat and cold blockers, but their effectiveness is directly related to quality. The best-quality shades, which are the most expensive, aid greatly in keeping an RV cooler in summer and warmer in winter. Some of the room-darkening shades block all light and have insulating properties, but others fall far short of total light blocking with a correspondingly lower insulating effect. An RV probably won't be equipped with true room-darkening shades, but they are available from places that sell residential shades.

Many RVs are either equipped with mini-blinds or the blinds are offered as options. We don't have mini-blinds for several reasons. They don't block all light and they can't be shut tightly enough to effectively provide insulation; cold and hot air can enter from between the slats and from the sides and bottom. Because RVs are smaller than residences, dust accumulates more quickly because it doesn't have the space to disperse; therefore, mini-blinds—with their multitude of dust-catching surfaces—need frequent cleaning. Mini-blinds on galley windows collect cooking grease, which is especially hard to clean. As full-timers, we don't want window coverings that need so much attention; we've always got better things to do than houseclean.

On some motorhomes, the mini-blinds rattle during travel. The only way to prevent this annoying noise is to raise the blinds.

Some luxury-model RVs are equipped with pleated fabric shades, the best being the day/night type. The "day" section admits a pleasant diffused light while affording total privacy. At night, the other more opaque section of the shade is used. Some pleated shades have a reflective backing that is as effective an insulator as a double-paned window. Pleated shades are fairly easy to keep clean; the best-quality shades are made of antistatic fabric that repels dust. When necessary, the shades can be cleaned with a vacuum or washed by hand.

Skylights are a feature of many new RVs. Sometimes the skylight is equipped with an adjustable covering, usually a pleated shade; if not, a shade should be installed. A skylight is a source of great heat loss in the winter and can warm the RV considerably in the summer if the sun is allowed to stream in.

"Live" in an RV Before Buying

With any RV you are considering, you should check it out by pretending to live in it. Try out the bed for size by lying down and stretching out on it. Check convertible sofas and dinettes to see if they are comfortable for sleeping. If you like to watch TV in bed, can you sit up comfortably while doing so? Sit on the toilet to see if there is enough knee room, then find out if you can get up easily. With your shoes off, step into the shower and go through the motions to see if it is practical for your use. Mentally store all the things you will carry in the RV to get an idea of whether the storage space is sufficient. Pretend to make a meal in the galley, especially where counter space is minimal.

Purchase the RV only if there are no problems, or if you can live with any you find. Unless you will be fulltiming, you may be able to accept the shortcomings because you will be living in the RV for only short periods.

Chapter 4

An RV's Systems

The utilities on most RVs provide the same conveniences as in a residence—hot and cold running water, electricity, and gas for cooking and heating—but the delivery systems are different than in household systems. To avoid problems, RVers should have a rudimentary knowledge about how the water, propane, and 12-volt direct current (DC) and 120-volt alternating current (AC) electrical systems work.

The Water System

In most RVs, the water system consists of an internal tank, electric water pump, and pipes running to the water heater, sinks, shower, and toilet. A pipe also runs to the connection that receives water from an external source (Figure 4-1). All waste water drains into holding tanks.

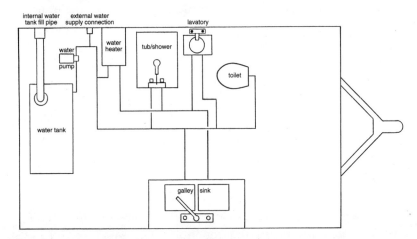

Figure 4-1. *The water system of a conventional trailer is shown here, but all types of trailers and motorhomes have a similar system.*

Potable Water

Potable water comes from either the internal tank or an outside water supply at the campsite. Campground water, whether it comes from the water company or a well, is referred to as "city water." It is fed to the RV by a hose (supplied by the RVer) attached to the campsite faucet and runs to the hose connection on the RV's exterior. The exterior connection joins to the line—from the internal tank and water pump—that feeds the water heater, toilet, sinks, and shower. All lines are plastic pipe and routed through cabinets and other storage areas, under the bed, and, rarely, under the floor.

The internal water tank is filled through a spout on the outside of the RV. The fill spout has a screw cap (and is usually in an enclosure with a locking door) to keep dirt and foreign objects out of the tank. It is large enough for a hose nozzle or funnel (which may be needed if the tank is filled using a water jug or other container).

When the RV is hooked up to city water, water from faucets has the same pressure as the city water. When water from the internal tank is used, a demand pump provides the pressurization. When the pump's master switch is on, the pump is activated as a faucet is opened, and water will flow. The master switch is always conveniently located: on the wall near the galley sink or incorporated into the monitor panel, which also has an illuminated readout of the water level in the tank. Some switches are lighted in the "on" position. When city water is used, the pump switch should be off. There are check valves in the lines near or at the city water connection and the water pump that prevent water from flowing in the wrong direction.

When the water supply comes from the internal tank and the RV is occupied, the pump switch should be on; however, it should be off when the RV is unoccupied. If a leak develops, the pump will run until all the water in the tank is pumped out—onto the floor; also, allowing the pump to run dry will ruin it. The switch should always be turned off when the RV is moving to prevent periodic cycling of the pump as the water surges back and forth in the tank and lines.

When city water is the source and a faucet is opened, there is no sound other than that of the water running; when the internal supply is used, either a steady or pulsating noise of the water pump is heard, depending on whether the faucet is fully or partially open. The noise is not loud or annoying because the water pump is installed where the sound is muffled, either near the water tank, in a cabinet, under the bed, or in a storage compartment. A pump "burping" every few seconds indicates that a faucet is not turned off all the way. When water is low in the internal tank, the sound of the pump changes noticeably; when the tank is almost dry, the pump chatters.

A water pump is a sealed unit that needs no maintenance other than occasional cleaning of the in-line filter. Irregular water pressure is the first sign that the filter needs cleaning. The filter is in a clear casing on one end of the pump; on most installations it can be visually checked for blockage. In all our years of RVing we have never had to clean a filter, but we are extra careful to put only clear, clean water in our tank (this is discussed in Chapter 8). Another cause of low pressure is a leak in the system, but in this case you will probably notice the burping of the pump before you are aware of the low pressure.

In some small folding tent trailers, pickup campers, and van conversions, the water system may consist of an internal tank with a water line to the sink, where the faucet is operated by a hand pump.

In all but top-of-the-line models, RV faucets are usually the two-handle type, but residential single-lever–type faucets can be installed on most RVs with a water pump system. Be sure a new faucet's base is no larger than the one being replaced. The undersink plumbing can usually be connected easily to the pipes on residential-type faucets.

The only alteration we had to make when installing a single-lever faucet on our lavatory was to shorten the water lines slightly. A compression fitting rejoined each pipe where a section was cut out.

Most RV showers are equipped with a special type of two-handled faucet (Figure 4-2). The shower hose is attached to a fitting behind the spout. On top of the faucet is a diverter valve that, when pulled up, shuts off the flow to the spout

Figure 4-2. *When the knob in the center of the faucet is lifted, water is diverted from the faucet to the shower hose.*

and diverts it to the shower head on the end of the hose. The shower head has a button or dial to control the water flow.

Some luxury RVs have single-lever faucets in the shower, but most units don't have enough space behind the wall to accommodate the necessary plumbing.

Is a Water Treatment System Necessary?

Although the quality of some city water supplies is questionable or deteriorating, in our opinion, an elaborate water treatment system is not necessary. In our many years of vacationing and fulltiming, which has taken us to 48 states and much of Canada, we have encountered few problems with water supplies.

If you are more comfortable with a water treatment system that removes bacteria, rather than a simple filter that removes only sediment, odors, and chlorine taste, finding a system practical for RV use may be difficult since most are designed for residential use. These systems generally require considerable water and electricity to process a small amount of bacteria-free water; therefore, treated water would not be available when camping without hookups. All water treatment systems require frequent maintenance to prevent the growth of undesirable bacteria.

It makes no sense to install a system under the sink to treat galley water while the lavatory water, used for drinking and brushing teeth, remains untreated. The best place to install a water treatment system is in the water line after the junction between the water pump and the city water connection. In this location, all water used in the RV is treated, whether it comes from the campground hookup or the internal tank. Wherever a water treatment system is installed, storage space will be lost.

Water Heaters

Most RVs have a propane-fueled water heater with either a 6- or 10-gallon capacity. Some heaters must be lit manually; others have automatic ignition. The access door is usually on the street side; a grille in the door provides needed ventilation (Figure 4-3).

To light the manual type, move the valve control knob to the pilot setting. While depressing the button next to the knob, apply a spark or flame to the gas orifice of the pilot light. Continue depressing the button for about 30 seconds after the pilot is lit. When the button is released, the pilot should stay lit (if it doesn't, repeat the process).

Figure 4-3. *The grille in the water heater door provides ventilation.*

Turn the valve control knob to the "on" position and set the thermostat to the desired temperature. The burner should now light. (In the summer, the pilot alone keeps the water hot enough for us.) This is the basic lighting procedure for water heaters (and some other propane-operated equipment), but you should consult the instruction manual for your heater for the proper procedure.

Matches can be used for lighting, but it's easier and safer to use a spark gun, which creates a spark, or a gas match, which has a flame. Spark guns have replaceable flints. Gas matches are similar to cigarette lighters and are either refillable or disposable. RV supply and hardware stores carry both types.

If the pilot light goes out for any reason—a high wind may blow it out—a sensor cools down to a certain temperature and then shuts off the gas flow. A device that automatically reignites the pilot light can be installed on the heater valve.

The type of water heater without a pilot light has thermostat-controlled piezo-electric ignition (in which mechanical pressure exerted on a crystal results in a spark) for lighting the main burner. This type can be controlled by an on/off switch inside the RV.

Some water heaters can be operated with both propane and 120-volt electricity. When electricity is used, a coil heats the water; with propane, either a pilot light or a piezo-electric igniter controls the burner.

Six or 10 gallons of water is sufficient for a satisfying shower if the water is used judiciously and not run at full force during the entire shower. This technique works well: First, wet your body; then, using the button or dial on the shower head, turn off or reduce the water flow to a trickle while you soap; increase the flow to rinse. We have a 6-gallon tank and, using this method, we can take successive showers and not run out of hot water.

When the burner goes on, it can be heard inside the RV in the vicinity of the water heater. This noise is normally not disturbing; however, if the water heater is located under the bed, as it was in one of our trailers, the noise may bother you at first, but you should get used to it, as we did.

Holding Tanks

The smallest folding tent trailers, pickup campers, and van conversions may not have holding tanks, but larger RVs usually have two tanks: one for gray water and one for black. Tank capacities generally increase in proportion to the RV's size. Because sinks and showers generate more waste than toilets, the gray-water tank may be the larger of the two, but some RVs have tanks of equal capacities.

Holding tanks in some RVs are in an enclosed compartment under the floor and receive heat from the furnace, thereby preventing winter freeze-ups. Holding tanks that aren't enclosed and heated are susceptible to freezing in cold weather, especially during travel.

Discharging the contents of holding tanks is controlled by a gate valve installed in the pipe from each tank. Beyond the valves, the pipes are connected to a T or Y fitting so the two tanks empty through a common pipe. On the end of this pipe is a fitting for attaching the sewer hose; when connected, the valves can be opened to empty the tanks (this procedure is explained in Chapter 8). The valves, usually located just under the bottom of the RV on the street side, are identified with labels indicating which tank each controls. Some RVs have a separate sewer discharge pipe for each holding tank, which necessitates shifting the sewer hose from one pipe to the other to empty both tanks.

Most RVs with holding tanks have a monitor panel with lights that indicate the liquid level of each tank. Electronic sensors attached at various points on one side of each tank provide readings that register whether the tank is empty, one- or two-thirds full (or one-quarter, one-half, or three-quarters full), or full. We've never had a monitor panel that gives truly accurate readings, but after spending some time living in the RV, it's easy to estimate tank levels.

A bubble forming in the toilet when the trap is opened indicates that the holding tank is getting full. When the gray-water tank is full, water backs up into the galley sink, lavatory, or shower drain, whichever is lowest or nearest to the holding tank.

Most of the water that goes into the gray-water tank is from showers. Using the shower-head button or dial to reduce water usage avoids filling the tank too quickly.

When the RV is not hooked up to a sewer, both valves are kept closed until the tanks are emptied at a dump station or into a sewer hookup at the next campsite. When staying for a few days or longer in a campsite with a sewer hookup, the procedure is different. With the sewer hose in place, the valve on the gray-water holding tank is left open so the waste water runs out. The black-water tank, however, should be emptied only every three or four days to allow enough liquid to accumulate to flush out the solids.

After emptying the black water and while the valve is still open, flush the toilet for a few seconds to rinse the tank and sewer hose. Once the black-water tank is empty, close the valve until the next dumping. Always close the gray-water valve before dumping the black water to prevent it from entering the gray-water tank. The valves to both holding tanks should never be open at the same time. Our practice is to close the gray-water valve about a day before dumping the black water, so once the black-water tank is emptied, the gray water flushes the sewer hose.

On some RVs, the shower water drains into the black-water tank. Evidently the manufacturers think they are doing RVers a favor by ensuring plenty of liquid to flush out the tank. A black-water tank with this arrangement fills very quickly.

Some campgrounds don't have a sewer drain at each site but have a special drain for gray water only. Sometimes gray water can be drained onto the ground, but this is allowed in only a few campgrounds. If the shower water, which constitutes the bulk of gray water, drains into the black-water tank, it can be disposed of only in a sewer.

On RVs without holding tanks, gray water from the sink usually runs out through a drain hose. It can be collected in a bucket, or a garden hose can be attached to the drain hose to run the gray water into a sewer hookup. If such an RV has a toilet, it's likely a portable type that must be removed to be emptied.

Toilets

RV toilets operate differently than residential toilets. Flushing is controlled by either a pedal near the base of the toilet or a lever on the side or at the back of the seat. Raising the pedal or pushing the lever in the opposite direction than for flushing keeps the trap closed while allowing water to enter the bowl. Some models have two pedals: one for flushing, the other for adding water.

When the toilet is flushed, city water or water from the internal tank enters the bowl through holes under the rim, and a trap in the bottom of the bowl opens. The flushing action of RV toilets is not as efficient as in residential toilets because they have a built-in water tank that provides several gallons of swirling, gravity-propelled water to rinse the bowl. Some RV toilets have a spray attachment that can be used to direct water into the bowl for rinsing.

After flushing, a small amount of water collects in the bowl once the trap is closed. Some water should remain to keep the seals lubricated, but make sure the water is low enough that it won't slosh out when the RV is moving.

Most standard RV toilets are box-shaped and made of plastic, but porcelain models resembling residential toilets may be available as an option. A standard toilet seat can be used on the larger porcelain models, but plastic models have somewhat smaller seats, so replacements have to be purchased from RV supply stores. (We mention this because we have had to replace the seats of plastic toilets when they cracked.)

The Propane System

Propane, or liquefied petroleum (LP) gas, is the fuel used for an RV's range, furnace, and water heater, and is one source of energy for the refrigerator (the other being electricity). The RVer is responsible for having a cylinder filled when it runs out of propane. Propane is sold at some service stations and convenience stores, always at bulk propane suppliers, and at some campgrounds.

The propane is stored in a cylinder (also called a bottle or a tank) with capacities from 5 gallons for small RVs to 50 gallons for the largest motorhomes. Cylinders are installed horizontally or vertically, and they should always be used, stored, or transported in the position for which they were designed.

Small RVs may have space for only one cylinder; two cylinders are usually standard equipment on larger RVs. It's handy to have two cylinders because, when one runs out, the gas is automatically switched over to the other (which should be kept full), providing an uninterrupted supply. The empty cylinder can be refilled at your convenience, but don't wait until the second cylinder runs out.

Because pressure in the tank drops as gas is used, all RV cylinders are equipped with a two-stage regulator to maintain the flow at the proper operating pressure (Figure 4-4). The regulator is located between the cylinders on a two-cylinder installation.

The screw valve on the top of each cylinder should be open; then, when one cylinder is empty, the regulator automatically switches over to the full one. The regulator has a knob with an arrow, which should always point toward the cylinder in use. When the regulator switches over, manually turn the knob so the arrow points to the full cylinder; then close the valve on the empty cylinder. (To open a valve, turn the handle counterclockwise; to close, turn it clockwise. You should be able to do this easily by hand. If a wrench is needed to turn the valve, it needs to be repaired or replaced.) If the arrow is always pointed at the cylinder in use, you will know when that cylinder is empty because the window on the regulator will be red (it's clear when there is propane in the cylinder). Check every few days to see if a cylinder has become empty.

On conventional trailers, the cylinders are mounted in front, on the wide part of the V-shaped rails that form the trailer's tongue. Some manufacturers enclose the cylinders in a rigid cover that slips off for access (Figure 4-5); on some conventional trailers a cylinder compartment is molded into the front.

The cylinders on fifth-wheel trailers are mounted in an outside compartment on one side of the trailer near the front or under the gooseneck. It's difficult to

Figure 4-4. *All RV propane cylinders require a regulator to control the pressure. Shown is a two-stage regulator, which does the job more efficiently than a single-stage regulator.*
(Courtesy Marshall Gas Controls)

remove an empty cylinder from a compartment under the goose-neck, and even more difficult to replace the heavier, filled cylinder.

Most trailer cylinders are the vertical type, and all are removable. Motorhomes may have a single horizontal cylinder permanently installed on the vehicle's frame. Since the cylinder can't be removed, the motorhome must be driven to where it can be refilled, which is a nuisance if you have to break camp just to get more propane.

Figure 4-5. *On some conventional trailers, the tongue-mounted propane cylinders are enclosed in a cover.*

To disconnect the cylinder from the regulator, simply unscrew the flexible hose, or pigtail, from the cylinder's valve. On the end of the pigtail is a POL (petroleum, oil, and lubricants) connection that screws into the cylinder's valve. An open-end or crescent wrench is needed to remove this connection, or an inexpensive plastic wrench (available from RV supply stores) that remains in place on the connection, and is easily turned by hand, can be used. With this type of wrench, the POL fitting tightens down on an O-ring (extra O-rings are stored in compartments in the wrench) for a leak-proof seal. No O-ring is involved when using a regular wrench, so the fitting must be snugged down well to prevent leaking. Since the fitting has a left-hand thread, it is turned clockwise for loosening, and counterclockwise for tightening (when facing the valve). The plastic wrench has arrows indicating connecting and disconnecting directions.

Never transport a vertical cylinder horizontally, or a horizontal cylinder vertically, to avoid the icing that may occur in the tubes in the tank.

Wherever the cylinders are mounted there must be adequate ventilation. The cylinder compartment has a door with many vents or a sizable grille. In addition, there is an opening in the bottom, so if a leak occurs, the gas will flow out of the compartment because it is heavier than air. Never put anything in the cylinder compartment that could block the vent openings.

As with holding tanks, you will develop a sense of when a propane cylinder is about to run out. We have two 7-gallon cylinders. In very cold weather when the furnace is used for heat, one cylinder lasts about a week. In the summer, when propane is used only for the water heater, cooking, and maybe a few days of operating the refrigerator, a cylinder lasts a month or longer.

Heating with Propane

Except for some large motorhomes that have a hot-water system to heat the interior, most RVs have a forced-air furnace that operates on propane. Small RVs may have a furnace with a fan that circulates warm air, while larger RVs typically have a furnace with a blower that forces the heated air through ducts running to all parts of the RV. Both furnace types must be vented to the outside.

Older small RVs may have a convection furnace, which has no fan to circulate the hot air. The furnace is usually mounted near the floor at the midpoint of the RV so both the front and rear receive some heat. This type of furnace is lit using the same procedure for lighting a propane water heater.

Even the smallest furnaces in today's RVs are likely to be thermostat-controlled. The thermostats resemble residential thermostats and operate in the same manner: The furnace is started by turning on the thermostat's switch and adjusting the temperature lever.

The furnace can be run as often as necessary when the RV is hooked up to shore power, but it must be used sparingly when the RV is on battery power (this is discussed in the electrical systems section later in this chapter). To conserve the battery, some RVers who camp without hookups use

Figure 4-6. *A catalytic heater provides heat for an RV without using any electric power.*
(Courtesy U.S. Catalytic Corporation)

a catalytic heater to warm their units (Figure 4-6).

A catalytic heater, which is fueled by propane, is either wall-mounted with a propane line running to it, or portable, connected to its own tiny propane cylinder. A catalytic heater is flameless; heat is generated from a chemical reaction between the propane and oxygen that occurs in a platinum-impregnated pad.

Catalytic heat has a warming effect similar to the sun—constant, penetrating, and satisfying.

A catalytic heater is not vented to the outside and must not be used without a source of fresh air. *This type of heater depletes the oxygen in the RV, so a window or roof vent must be open whenever it is being used.*

The Galley Range

The galley range is also fueled by propane. It's similar to a residential gas range—about the size of an apartment range but with a smaller oven.

Some galley ranges are equipped with a pilot light, but most RVers use a spark or flame lighter to ignite the burners and oven, because a valve under the range top must be opened to use the pilot light and closed before the RV is moved. Not using the pilot saves on propane consumption, and doesn't contribute extra heat in hot weather.

To light the oven, first turn the thermostat knob to the pilot setting, then hold the lighter at the gas orifice—located under the lower shelf of the oven, toward the rear, in the center—until a flame appears. Adjust the thermostat to the desired temperature.

The Propane Mode of the Refrigerator

Before discussing propane refrigerators, a description of RV refrigerators is in order because they are different than residential models. Rather than the compressor type used in residences, in which the refrigerant is first compressed and then expanded for cooling, most RV refrigerators are the absorption type that use heat for cooling. Heat is absorbed from the interior of the box and transferred by tubing to the outside, where it is released; where there is no heat, there is cold. Absorption refrigeration is a simple system that has no moving parts.

RV refrigerators have cooling fins inside the box on the upper portion of the back wall. Over a period of use, ice builds up on the fins. Under the fins, a drip tray catches drops of water from the ice that melts when the refrigerator door is open. A projection on the back of the tray fits over a drain. Water in the tray drains into a container on the back of the refrigerator, where it eventually evaporates. The drip container, the condenser coils, and the burner are located in an outside compartment with a ventilated door.

A sizable vent in the roof above the refrigerator compartment dissipates heat from the absorption process. Absorption-type refrigerators are not self-defrosting. (Methods of defrosting are discussed in Chapter 10.)

Many RV refrigerators can be operated on either 120-volt electricity—the type supplied by a campground's electric hookup—or propane. Refrigerators in motorhomes may be three-way automatic energy selector (AES) models that are operated on either 120- or 12-volt electricity or propane. Some small refrigerators used in van conversions and pickup campers are the compressor type, which operate on either type of electricity but not propane. (The electrical operation of refrigerators is discussed later in this chapter.)

Most refrigerators in new and recent-model RVs are automatic; to operate them on propane requires nothing more than switching to that mode. The switch is on the eyebrow panel (the panel at the top of the refrigerator), along with the thermostat control; "LP" or "gas" is illuminated on the panel when the refrigerator is operating on propane.

To light some older refrigerators, a button that controls the gas valve is pushed in and held while an ignitor button is repeatedly pushed until a flame is visible in a viewing prism; the valve button is then held down for about 30 seconds. When the button is released, a visible flame indicates that the pilot has ignited. As with the water heater, if the flame doesn't stay on when the button is released (it usually does), the process must be repeated. Instead of a viewing prism, some refrigerators have a light that flashes until the pilot is lit.

The 120-Volt Alternating Current Electrical System

Of an RV's two electrical systems, the 120-volt alternating current (AC) system (the power provided by a campground electric hookup, often referred to as shore power) is the easiest to understand because it's the same type of electricity as that supplied to residences. When an RV is hooked up to shore power, electricity use is the same as at home: Electrical equipment is plugged into the handiest receptacle; that's all there is to it. Most RVs have several receptacles; probably one in the galley, one adjacent to the bath lavatory, one in the dining area, one or more in both the living room and bedroom, and one on the exterior.

The refrigerator, air conditioner, and microwave oven (if the RV is so equipped) do not have to be plugged in for use. Their receptacles are wired into the system and the items remain plugged into their respective receptacles. An air conditioner's receptacle is inside the unit's covering and is not visible; the microwave's receptacle is usually inside a cabinet adjacent to the microwave; and the refrigerator's receptacle is in the outside compartment behind the refrigerator.

A master circuit breaker controls the AC system. It must be in the "on" position for the RV to receive power. The air conditioner and microwave typically share one circuit, but the refrigerator and converter/charger (discussed later in this chapter) are usually on separate circuits. Depending on the size of the RV, the receptacles may be on one or more circuits; large units may have many circuits.

Each circuit is protected by a circuit breaker that trips, or shuts off the circuit, when an abnormal electrical condition occurs, the most common of which is overloading. Switching the breaker back on won't do any good unless the load is reduced (see Chapter 8 for how to avoid overloading).

Ground Fault Circuit Interrupters

A receptacle near a water source may have a built-in ground fault circuit interrupter (GFCI), a safety device that shuts off the current if an unsafe condition is present in the circuit, thus preventing the user of the receptacle from receiving an electrical shock. When the button in the center of the receptacle pops out, the circuit is turned off. Dampness or wetness often causes a temporary problem. Sometimes an inside GFCI receptacle and an outside receptacle are on the same circuit; when it rains, an electrical leakage may occur, causing the button to pop out. After the wet condition clears up, reset the GFCI by pushing the button back in; if the button won't stay in, a problem still exists in the circuit and an electrician may have to fix it.

Generators

On some RVs, a generator supplies 120-volt electricity when the RV isn't hooked up to shore power. On many motorhomes, a generator is standard equipment; if not, usually the option is available. If, at the time of purchase, you are undecided about a generator, it can probably be added later because almost all motorhomes (but only a few large trailers) have a prewired generator compartment.

A motorhome's generator is primarily used to run the roof air conditioner while traveling. The dashboard air conditioner can't begin to cool the interior of most motorhomes. In cool weather, the generator can power an electric heater to supplement the automotive heater. (If an electric heater is used during travel, it should be secured so that it can't move or tip over.) A heat strip can be added to some air conditioners and used for supplemental heat while the motorhome is under way. A heat strip is not practical for general heating because hot air rises; with the hot air already at ceiling level, the floor area won't receive enough heat.

A generator provides 120-volt AC electricity just as shore power does, but, unlike shore power, a generator is best used for only high-wattage items (see Table 8-1, page 168); it's very expensive to use for running a power tool or other low-wattage items. It's more economical to use low-wattage items when the generator is already powering a high-wattage item.

Because noise is a problem with generators, their operation is prohibited in most private campgrounds; when operation is allowed in public (or private) campgrounds, the hours of operation may be restricted.

Inverters

Inverters are another means of obtaining 120-volt AC power when the RV is not plugged into an external power outlet. Inverters convert 12-volt DC battery power into 120-volt AC power, but they do so at a cost: a large drain on the battery. To successfully use an inverter, the RV should have at least two batteries.

Unlike generators, inverters are best for small loads. They are also easier to install and are completely silent when operating. In trailers, it is often more practical to install an inverter than a generator. TVs in motorhomes are often powered by a small, or pocket, inverter.

The 12-Volt Direct Current Electrical System

Of all the systems in an RV, the 12-volt direct current (DC) system is the least understood, probably because there is no residential counterpart. If you are new to RVing, you may think you are unfamiliar with this system; however, it is the same electrical system as in automobiles.

The RV's Batteries

An RV's 12-volt electrical system is powered by a deep-cycle battery, called the house battery. It provides the power for all 12-volt items: the interior and exterior lights, the water pump, the furnace blower, the range hood fan, the vent fan in the bath, the electronic ignition on some water heaters and refrigerators, and the 12-volt mode on an AES refrigerator. In addition to the house battery, motorhomes have another battery for the automotive functions: an SLI (starting/lights/ignition) battery, the type also used in automobiles, vans, and pickup trucks.

While both types of batteries are similar in appearance and function—providing power for a 12-volt system—they are constructed and perform the function differently. The SLI battery is designed to provide for the short surges of considerable power needed to start a vehicle's engine. SLI batteries are rated by their cold-cranking amperes (amps), the number of amps available to start an engine at a cold temperature. The larger the engine, the more amps it needs to crank it over for starting. The SLI battery is designed to be slightly discharged and quickly recharged many times. The vehicle's alternator takes care of the recharging and also maintains the battery at the proper level of charge during driving.

The most common SLI batteries are maintenance-free, or sealed, which means no fluid ever needs to be added to the cells. Less common nowadays are wet-cell SLI batteries, which need to have fluid (usually distilled water) added periodically.

Unlike an SLI battery, a deep-cycle battery is constructed to be slowly and deeply discharged, and slowly recharged many times. Some deep-cycle batteries are maintenance-free, but most are the wet-cell type that need the same maintenance as a wet-cell SLI battery. If your RV has wet-cell batteries, they should be (but sometimes aren't) located for easy inspection and servicing. Some larger RVs have house batteries in a compartment on a sliding tray—a very convenient arrangement.

SLI and deep-cycle batteries should not be interchanged. A vehicle's engine would start using a deep-cycle battery and an RV's DC circuits would work off an SLI battery, but neither battery would last long if used for these purposes. The only batteries that should be used for house batteries are labeled "RV/marine deep cycle."

Deep-cycle batteries carry a group designation; Group 24 and

Group 27 are the most common. They may have a cold-cranking amps rating, but it is a useless rating for deep-cycle batteries; meaningful ratings are amp-hour (Ah) capacity and reserve capacity, although neither of these ratings may appear on the battery. A Group 24 battery has a capacity range of 70 to 85 amp-hours; a Group 27, 90 to 105 amp-hours. What this translates to in terms of RV usage is that, in theory, a 105-amp-hour battery will run a light drawing 1 amp—approximately the amperage of a common 12-volt RV interior light—for 105 hours, or two lights for 52.5 hours, and so on.

The reserve capacity (based on the length of time the battery delivers a 25-amp load) is expressed in minutes and is another indication of amp-hour capacity. A Group 24 battery's reserve capacity is 120 to 130 minutes; for a Group 27 battery, it is 160 to 175 minutes. (Reserve capacity in minutes multiplied by 0.65 equals approximate amp-hours.)

Batteries with the most minutes of reserve capacity provide power to run a given electrical item for a longer time than a battery with fewer minutes.

If your RVing lifestyle involves spending each night in a campground with an electric hookup, or if you have a small RV, you can probably get by with just one house battery. If you ever intend to spend any time camping without an electric hookup, and the length of your RV is 23 feet or longer, it's much more convenient to have two batteries. The number and size of the batteries that can be installed, however, depends entirely on the size of the battery box. Smaller RVs usually have space for one house battery; most mid-size and large RVs have space for two (although we have seen very large RVs with room for only one). Many battery boxes designed to hold two batteries accommodate only two Group 24s instead of the slightly larger Group 27s. Measure the box before purchasing Group 27 batteries to be sure they will fit.

Recharging the Battery.   An RV is wired so that when a motorhome, pickup camper, or camping van conversion is driven or a trailer is towed, the house battery is recharged by the vehicle's alternator. In self-propelled RVs, the wiring from the alternator goes directly to the house battery. In a trailer, the wiring connection is made when the trailer electrical connector cable (TECC is our acronym) on a conventional trailer's tongue, or a fifth-wheeler's kingpin box, is plugged into its socket on the tow vehicle. For conventional trailers, this socket is normally located under the tow vehicle's rear bumper to the left of the hitch receiver. With a fifth-wheel trailer, the socket is near the hitch, which necessarily must be in the bed of a pickup. The TECC is either a seven- or nine-pin plug and contains the wiring connections for the trailer's running and brake lights, turn signals, electric brakes, and, on the nine-pin version, the backup lights.

After an overnight stay without an electric hookup, the battery may be considerably discharged, and it can take hours of driving to fully recharge it. How efficiently the battery is recharged depends on the size of the alternator and the length and size of the wire between the house battery and the alternator. Large motorhomes usually have a high-output alternator with adequate wiring, and the batteries are in close proximity. This enables the house battery to recharge very quickly during driving.

If a tow vehicle has a good-size alternator (90-amp output or more), adequate wiring in the charge line, and batteries located at or near the front of the trailer, the same quick charging can result. Only new full-size pickup trucks, however, have an alternator with an output high enough to recharge batteries in a short period, and most systems do not have wiring heavy enough for the charge line to do the job. If any part of the charge system isn't adequate, it may take hours of driving to recharge the batteries.

A few years ago some manufacturers placed the battery compartments at the rear of their trailers. It is unlikely that batteries in this location could ever be recharged even if you drove all day. On trailers, the battery compartment should be as close to the alternator as possible; that means at the front of the trailer.

Recharging during driving is important if you spend a night without an electric hookup and the next camping place will also be without hookups. You will want to recharge the house batteries as quickly as possible for the second night's usage. Charging the batteries during driving is not so critical if the subsequent stop has an electric hookup.

The Converter/Charger

Almost all RVs with 120- and 12-volt systems are equipped with a converter/charger (Figure 4-7), although it may be an option on some smaller RVs. When an RV is connected to a 120-volt AC source, the

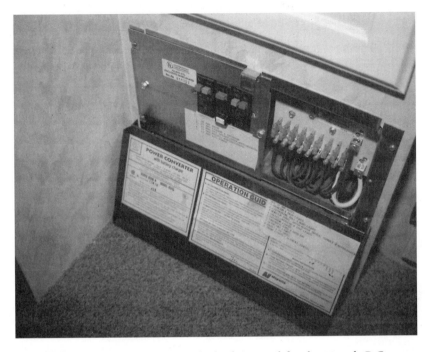

Figure 4-7. *A converter/charger with the fuse panel for the 12-volt DC system (on the right) and the AC circuit breakers (on the left).*

converter/charger, a component of the RV's AC system, is automatically activated. Briefly, this is how a converter/charger functions: It operates on 120-volt AC electricity and, when connected to a shore-power source or a suitable generator, as 12-volt equipment is used, the converter automatically supplies power for the equipment without any battery discharge. At the same time, the charger recharges the batteries, if necessary. This is why recharging batteries while driving is not too important if you have an electric hookup at your next overnight stop. Although the converter/charger is a complex electronic device, its operation is usually trouble-free, it needs no maintenance, and it probably will last for many years.

A few RVs may have a unit that is only a converter. With a converter, if you arrive at a campground with a depleted battery, the battery will not be recharged because the voltage output of a converter is just slightly higher than that of a fully charged battery (12.7 volts), thus not enough to effect a charge. As long as shore power is available, however, the battery will not be depleted further. The charger in a converter/

charger is a true battery charger and delivers a voltage high enough (13.8 volts) to recharge the battery.

Before you go boondock camping, make sure you know whether your RV is equipped with a converter/charger or just a converter; it can make a difference when it comes time to properly recharge the battery.

Plugging into shore power when a battery is considerably discharged may put too much initial load on the converter/charger and cause its internal circuit breaker to trip. It will reset itself and perhaps go through several cycles of tripping and resetting before it settles down. A slight hum is the only noise a converter/charger or converter is likely to make; in many models, the hum is not noticeable.

The Fuse Panel

Another component of an RV's 12-volt system is the fuse, or circuit breaker, panel. Some newer RVs have the fuse panel incorporated in the converter/charger (see Figure 4-7). Know where the panel is located and, if it's the fuse type, always keep a supply of spare fuses of all amperage ratings used.

If the circuits are unlabeled on the panel, pull each fuse or trip each breaker, check what isn't working, and then label the circuit accordingly. For example, if after you remove a fuse or trip a breaker, all the 12-volt equipment works except the water pump, the water pump would be on that circuit. It is common for all lights on one side of the RV to be on one circuit. The furnace and water pump may be on separate circuits.

If a fuse blows or a breaker trips, a simple glitch or temporary condition may be the cause. Simply replacing the fuse or resetting the breaker may correct the condition. If replacement fuses continue to blow or the circuit breaker repeatedly trips, a serviceperson may have to correct the problem.

Using the 12-Volt System

On the first few nights of operating on battery power, it is not unusual for new RVers to overuse the 12-volt equipment, thus causing a considerable discharge of the battery. You will know when the battery is getting low if the lights become dimmer later in the evening or the water pump delivers water slower or sounds sluggish. If the battery dies, you would have no lights, which might be a minor inconvenience, but unless you had an alternate supply of water, you would have to go without because there is no practical way to get water from the tank without the electric pump.

A common problem for motorhomers, especially those with children, is excessive use of the dashboard stereo when the engine isn't running. As in other automotive vehicles, the dashboard stereo is powered by the SLI battery. If the stereo is used for hours, the SLI battery may be depleted so much that the motorhome's engine won't start. A portable stereo is better for boondock-camping entertainment. After a few nights of camping without an electric hookup, you will learn to gauge your use of 12-volt equipment to avoid a discharged battery.

If you have an RV with an AES refrigerator (this type is not often installed in trailers), never operate it on 12-volt power when the RV is parked; this depletes the battery very quickly. The 12-volt mode of a refrigerator should be used only during travel—when the engine of the RV is running—the theory being that the engine's alternator, not the battery, will supply the power.

An AES refrigerator running in the 12-volt mode draws considerable current. The alternator must have an amperage output high enough to handle this current along with all other 12-volt automotive loads. In some vehicles, the alternator is not large enough, so the house battery provides the extra current needed and could be considerably discharged after a few hours of driving with the refrigerator running.

For fast recharging and to extend its life, a deep-cycle battery should never be discharged to more than 50 percent of its amp-hour capacity. For a Group 24 battery, this is about 35 to 40 amp-hours; 50 percent of capacity of a Group 27 battery is about 45 to 50 amp-hours. Calculating this can be done by using Table 4-1, which lists the amperage draw of common 12-volt items, and Table 4-2, which shows how the figures can be used to arrive at the total amperage draw of 12-volt equipment used on a typical overnight stay.

The amperage for interior lights is an average: Three or four lights may be on for varying times or one light may be on for a specific period. Water pump use is intermittent, so the total for the whole time has to be estimated. It's best to avoid extended showers and running the furnace for long periods when operating on battery power.

For more information about RV 120-volt AC and 12-volt DC systems, consult *RV Electrical Systems: A Basic Guide to Troubleshooting,*

Table 4-1. Hourly Amperage Draw of 12-Volt RV Equipment

Equipment	Amps
Incandescent light, single socket, Type 1141 bulb	1.5
Incandescent light, double socket, Type 1141 bulb	2.5
Incandescent light, single socket, Type 1003 bulb	0.9
Incandescent light, double socket, Type 1003 bulb	1.8
Fluorescent light, single tube, 8-watt	0.7
Fluorescent light, single tube, 15-watt	1.2
Fluorescent light, double tube, 30-watt	2.0
Water pump	4.0 to 8.0
Forced-air furnace	5.0 to 8.0
Roof vent fan, 3-speed (depending on brand and speed)	1.8 to 7.3
Bath vent fan	2.0
Range hood fan	2.0
Refrigerator, 12-volt DC, compressor type	6.0
Refrigerator, 3-way (AES), on 12-volt setting	15.0 to 35.0
TV, AC/DC, 9-inch, color, on DC	3.0 to 4.0
TV, AC/DC, 5-inch, black and white, on DC	1.0 to 1.5
Stereo/cassette player, automotive type	1.7 to 6.0
Equalizer/amplifier on stereo/cassette player	1.0 to 2.0
CB radio, receive-only mode	0.5
Video cassette player, 12-volt	1.5

Table 4-2. Daily Amp-Hour Consumption

Equipment	Amp-Hours
Three lights for 4 hours (4 hours x 4.5 amps)	18.00
Water pump for 45 minutes; includes two showers (0.75 hour x 5 amps)	3.75
TV, color, for 2 hours (2 hours x 4 amps)	8.00
Miscellaneous (clock, LED pilot lights, etc.)	2.00
Total amp-hours used in a 24-hour period	31.75

Note:
   All figures are approximate and are based on typical amp-hour usage.

Repairs, and Improvement by Bill and Jan Moeller (Ragged Mountain Press, P.O. Box 220, Camden, Maine 04843).

The TV System

Most recent RVs have built-in provisions for a TV system, consisting of an antenna (sometimes an option), one or two antenna connections, and one or two 12-volt outlets. If there are two connections, one will be in the living room and the other in the bedroom.

The antenna is generally mounted on the roof. Most RV antennas are designed to be raised for use and lowered for travel; however, some motorhomes and van conversions have a fixed antenna so passengers can watch TV while traveling. Fixed antennas are either boomerang-shaped or circular.

The control for raising and lowering an antenna is on the ceiling, usually in the living room. A handle is turned in one direction for raising and the opposite for lowering. The handle or a small circular plate is pulled down and rotated to point the antenna in the desired direction. A TV's built-in antenna doesn't work well inside the metal skin of an RV, so a roof antenna is necessary for decent reception.

Because so many campgrounds now offer cable TV, most recent-model RVs have a cable connection on the exterior, usually on the street side.

Unless the dealer installs a TV as an option, you will need an antenna cable to hook up the TV. (Radio Shack is a good source for antenna cables, but they are found wherever TV accessories are sold.) The antenna hookup will be the same as with a house antenna. Adapters can be purchased if the antenna cable's fittings aren't compatible with your TV or the RV's antenna connection.

An amplifier, used to improve reception from distant stations, will be located near the TV; it may be on the same receptacle as a 12-volt socket. The best amplifiers have a built-in on/off switch; the amplifier should be turned off when tuned to local channels to avoid a degraded picture from over-amplification.

On RVs with a built-in exterior connection for cable TV, the amplifier has an additional switch to select either the antenna or the cable signal input.

A built-in amplifier may be incorporated in some TV antennas. The on/off switch will be on either the ceiling or the wall near the antenna control.

To avoid damage, the amplifier should be turned off during electrical storms. If there is no amplifier on/off switch, put the antenna/cable TV input switch on the cable setting for the duration of the storm and don't use the TV.

AC/DC TVs, sometimes with a built-in VCR, are available. Dual-voltage TVs can be used on battery power when you camp without an electric hookup.

In the RV, the 12-volt connection for an AC/DC TV is a cigarette-lighter–type socket, which accommodates the plug on the TV's 12-volt cord.

Table 4-1 lists a 12-volt TV's current requirements; adjust your usage accordingly when operating on DC to avoid excessive battery discharge.

Know How to Operate Your RV Equipment

Never leave the dealer's lot with your new (or new to you) RV without knowing how to operate all the equipment. The workings of the water heater, furnace, range, refrigerator, air conditioner, and generator (if there is one) should all be demonstrated. Know where the water pump switch, TV antenna control, propane supply, fuse or circuit breaker panel, and battery are located. Have the water, electric, and sewer hookup procedures explained, and know where the hookup equipment and connections are located. If the RV is equipped with an awning, learn how to set it up and put it away. Beginning trailerists should have the hitching procedure demonstrated. The setting-up and breaking-down procedures for a folding tent trailer or any unit with a pop-top also should be demonstrated.

If you don't fully understand any procedure, have it repeated until you do. Many dealers ask buyers to sign a form indicating that all equipment was working properly and operating procedures were demonstrated. Your signature on this form may have a bearing on warranty work to correct problems occurring after you take delivery, as well as dealer liability regarding any installation problems.

Some dealers don't pay enough attention to this aspect of selling an RV, and some new owners may not insist on a thorough briefing.

How do we know? Because new RV owners frequently come to our door to ask for help with equipment they don't know how to operate. We have shown them how to light stoves and water heaters, turn on furnaces, operate combination propane/electric refrigerators and water heaters, locate sewer hose and shore-power cable storage compartments, and track down the fuse panel to replace blown fuses.

Be sure you receive instruction manuals for all equipment—not only for later reference, but also for warranty information. Also make sure you receive an owner's manual from the RV manufacturer.

Further Checking-out Procedures

As soon as practical after taking delivery of your RV, use every system, not just once but several times. Light all propane appliances and let them run for a while. Check if the water heater heats properly and doesn't leak, the furnace cycles on and off according to the thermostat setting, the refrigerator cools enough, the oven reaches the proper temperature (check it with an oven thermometer), the stove's burners are adjusted correctly, and there is no smell of propane, which indicates a leak.

To check for leaks, put a little dishwashing liquid in some water in a bowl and use a soft brush or rag to apply the solution to all propane connections. Bubbles appear where there is a leak. If the connectors aren't the source of the leak, it may be a crack in the copper propane lines. Coat the lines with the soap solution to find the leak. NEVER CHECK FOR LEAKS WITH AN OPEN FLAME.

Turn on all faucets to make sure the water pump is working, the water is flowing properly (one of our trailers had manufacturing debris lodged in a pipe, partially blocking the flow), there are no leaks, and that the faucets shut off completely. Also check the water system of the toilet.

Operate all electrical systems, both 120-volt AC and 12-volt DC. Improperly installed electrical connections can come loose from movement of the RV (on another trailer of ours, two connectors fell off, evidently while in transit to the dealer). See that the refrigerator cools in the electric mode and that the water heater, if it is a propane/electric model, functions properly in the electric mode. Turn on every light, inside and out. Check the air conditioner, the range hood fan, and any roof vent fans.

Open and shut all windows and vents. Make sure entry and compartment doors open and close properly. Be sure latches on cabinets aren't broken; the latches on some units aren't very sturdy.

Inspect the underside of the RV for openings around plumbing where rodents can enter. We had to rid our previous trailer of half a dozen field mice before we located and sealed a gap around the shower drain.

With a hose, spray closed windows, doors, roof vents, and around the TV antenna to locate any leaks.

Ideally, make these inspections before you leave on a trip so you won't have to deal with problems while you are on the road. Unfortunately, many RVers don't take the time to check out a unit thoroughly until they are actually using it.

Another reason to check out your RV systems and equipment as soon as possible is to ensure they are working properly before warranties expire. If you can't get away to check out your RV, consider living in it in your own driveway for a time.

Trailerists need to road test their units to check the trailer brakes and running lights; motorhomers need to use their units on the road to determine whether the engine and other automotive systems are functioning properly.

 *Chapter 5*

Trip Planning

Much of the fun of RVing is in planning the trip, whether you are going away for a weekend or several weeks. Unless you are a fulltimer, chances are your trip will be limited to a certain period of time. A job may dictate your time off, or obligations such as school openings may determine how long you can stay away. To make the most of long or short vacations, some advance planning is in order. You will need maps, campground directories, and perhaps tour guides for the places you intend to visit, and you may want to join a club or organization that offers planning and on-the-road assistance.

Travel-related Clubs and Organizations

Before taking off on a trip, it may be worthwhile to join an automobile club. If you have an oil company credit card, you have probably received information about its auto club. Road maps and emergency road service are typical benefits. Your vehicle insurance company may also have an auto club.

Inquire about the towing feature of any road service, especially as it applies to RVs. Most auto clubs provide towing only for motorized vehicles; a motorhome or a tow vehicle would qualify, but a trailer would not. Sometimes only one vehicle is eligible for free towing, which means that those with motorhomes towing an auxiliary vehicle won't have coverage for both.

Evidently, road service planners must think it unlikely that a trailer would need to be towed, but it can happen. Once, when one of our trailer springs broke, we were only a block away from the campground where we intended to stay, so we managed to limp into it. We would have needed a tow had it happened anywhere else. In the event of a major accident, both the tow vehicle and trailer could be damaged, as could a motorhome and its dinghy.

Road service organizations specifically for RVers and who also cover any type of rig are advertised in RVing publications. An American Automobile Association (AAA) membership is valuable for travelers, but its RV towing service may be limited; check with your local AAA office for the policies in your state. Even if the towing service doesn't cover your needs, it may be worthwhile to join for the excellent trip-routing services; city, state, and regional maps; and tour books that are provided free to members.

Maps

Maps are an important traveling tool but many RVers don't use them to their best advantage because they are unaware of the wealth of information maps offer. A good map can make traveling easier and safer. You can find alternate routes when a main route can't be used, and they can spark your imagination and lead you to new discoveries. Poring over maps and searching for new roads to explore is one of our favorite pastimes.

Maps are easy to come by even though oil companies no longer give them away. Maps produced by Rand McNally, H. M. Gousha Company, and others can be purchased at service stations, convenience stores, bookstores, and many other outlets. Most state maps cost $2 or less; road atlases with maps of all the states are priced around $10. Free maps are a benefit to members of some auto and travel clubs.

Often the best map of a state is issued by the state tourism department. These maps are always free and chock-full of useful information, much of which isn't found on commercial maps. In addition to the map itself, there may be a section containing points of interest; a list of public parks and recreation areas, including campgrounds and their facilities; altitudes; radio stations; towns with hospitals; annual events; tolls for bridges, tunnels, and toll roads; ferry information; temperature tables; selected tours; ski areas; telephone numbers for emergencies and for travel information; and populations of major towns. State maps are available at visitor centers, chamber of commerce offices, and sometimes at campgrounds.

We always travel with two or three maps of the state we are in because the roads shown vary among mapmakers. We like to take the less traveled roads instead of rushing from point to point on interstate highways, so we want all the information we can get. We also use several maps because each has different features, such as more secondary roads or topographical indications.

To keep our maps handy for use, they are attached to a clipboard kept between us on the seat of our truck, and folded open to the section of the state in which we are traveling (Figure 5-1). On top of the pile is usually an AAA map, which we think is the easiest to read. A feature that contributes to their readability is the colors used: green areas denote forests, parks, and recreation areas; yellow shows city boundaries; and gray is used for topographical features. The main highways, printed in bright red, stand out against these pastel tints. Some state maps have such intense colors for every feature that nothing shows up well. We habitually track down historic sites, some rather obscure. We often use Gousha maps for this because they show more historic sites than any other maps we have found. We always try to have official state maps because they usually indicate every town and have street maps of both large and small towns.

AAA Triptik maps are quite useful. Printed in just red, black, and gray, these are easy-to-read strip maps of approximately 200-mile sections of interstate and major highways. It's easy to calculate mileage

Figure 5-1. *A clipboard is handy for keeping maps in the cockpit of a tow vehicle or motorhome.*

from either direction using the scale on each side of the strip. Exit numbers and symbols for services found at each exit are shown. Rest areas are clearly indicated. Because they are the size of a folded map, the small strips are easy to handle. All the strips for a trip are assembled in the order of travel and held together with a spiral binder.

For in-depth exploration of an area, county maps are available from county clerk offices. We purchased many of these maps in various parts of the country when we were doing genealogical research. A local historical society may also have useful maps for sale.

Since we like to take off on backwoods roads, we often augment our regular state maps with U.S. Forest Service or Bureau of Land Management (BLM) maps. They are sold in U.S. Forest Service and BLM offices.

A road atlas of all states is handy for trip planning, but the maps are usually too small to be useful when driving, and the book format doesn't make for easy handling in the cockpit.

Campgrounds

Once you have decided where to go, you will want to know campground locations along the way and at your destination. There are plenty to choose from since there are more than 16,000 campgrounds in the United States in every conceivable location: at seashores, in the mountains, in cities and hamlets, in rural areas, in forests, on the plains, and on rivers, streams, and lakes. Finding these campgrounds, however, is a worry to some new RVers. We are frequently asked how we locate places to camp. The answer is: We use campground directories.

Two large directories that cover public and private campgrounds in all the states, Canadian provinces, and Mexico are the *Trailer Life Campground and RV Services Directory* and *Woodall's Campground Directory*. They are for sale in RV supply stores, bookstores, and in the magazine section in some supermarkets and pharmacies. The directories also can be ordered: for *Woodall's*, call 1-800-323-9076; for *Trailer Life*, call 1-800-234-3450.

These all-encompassing directories are very thick, with more than 1,500 pages, but *Woodall's* offers eastern and western editions that are smaller and therefore easier to use and store. If your traveling is confined to one region, this type of directory may suffice.

Wheeler's RV Resort and Campground Guide is another directory that covers the United States, Canada, and Mexico, but it is about half the size of the *Trailer Life* and *Woodall's* directories and contains proportionately fewer listings. *Wheeler's* doesn't have quite the wide distribution of the other two, but it can be ordered by calling 1-800-323-8899. Updated editions of all three directories are published annually.

Free campground directories, published by many state tourism offices, are readily available. On an interstate highway, after crossing a state line, we stop at the welcome center to pick up the state map, brochures of interest, and the state campground directory. Sometimes the directory is available only from a staffperson on duty, and you may have to request it. These publications, as well as a local campground directory, may also be obtained at visitor centers or chamber of commerce offices.

To aid in trip planning, a tourism package that includes a state map can be ordered in advance. Addresses of state tourism offices are listed in the Appendix. When ordering, be sure to mention that you want RV campground information.

Whenever we see a rack of travel brochures, we look for those pertaining to campgrounds in the area and along the route we are taking. An extra benefit: Some brochures have a discount coupon. U.S. Forest Service and BLM offices have directories of the campgrounds in their districts, which indicate the campgrounds that have sites suitable for RVs.

The *Trailer Life* and *Woodall's* directories present the information in the same way: A state map is provided with symbols indicating the towns in which, or near which, campgrounds are located (Figure 5-2). A different symbol indicates where RV supplies and services are available. Individual campgrounds are listed in the main part of the directory, in the state section under the town's name.

Each listing contains basic information: the campground's name, street address, and phone number; whether the facility is public or private; directions to the campground; dates of operation; number of sites and how many are pull-throughs; available hookups and the amperage of the electric hookups (why this is important is explained in Chapter 8); the surface of the sites (paved, grass, gravel, or dirt); any restrictions on RV length; conveniences (dump station, laundry, recreational facilities); and rates (Figure 5-3). (*Woodall's* lists rates for only private campgrounds; *Wheeler's* doesn't include any rates.)

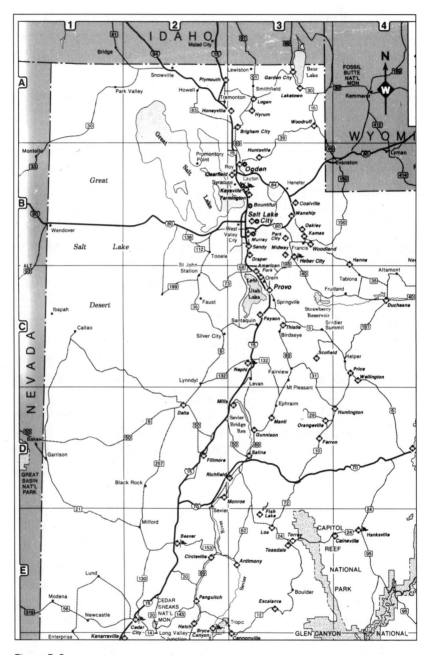

Figure 5-2. *A state map page from the* Woodall's Campground Directory. *A diamond-enclosed W indicates a town where campgrounds are located; a star with a dot in the center, an RV service center; and a flag marks a tourist attraction.* (Courtesy Woodall Publishing Company)

utah

All privately-owned campgrounds personally inspected by Woodall Representatives Dean & Donna McBride.

AMERICAN FORK—C-3

American Campground—Level, grassy & gravel sites with mountain view convenient to interstate. *From jct I-15 & Hwy 180 (American Fork/Pleasant Grove exit 279): Go 1/4 mi N on Hwy 180, then 100 yards W on 620 S St.* ◇◇FACILITIES: 52 sites, 52 full hookups, (20 & 30 amp receptacles), seasonal sites, 35 pull-thrus, flush toilets, hot showers, sewage disposal, laundry, public phone, LP gas refill by meter, tables. No tents. Open all year. Rate in 1993 $10-14.25 for 2 persons. Phone: (801) 756-5502. FCRV 10% discount.

UINTA NATIONAL FOREST (Granite Flat Campground)—*From jct US 89 & Hwy 74: Go 4 mi N on Hwy 74, then 7 mi E on Hwy 92 to FR 085, then 4 mi N on paved road.* FACILITIES: 32 sites, 25 ft. max RV length, 32 no hookups, tenting available, flush toilets, tables, fire rings, grills, wood. RECREATION: lake/river/stream fishing, hiking trails. Open late May through Sep 30. Phone: (801) 785-3563.

UINTA NATIONAL FOREST (Little Mill Campground)—*From jct US 89 & Hwy 74: Go 4 mi N on Hwy 74, then 6 mi E on Hwy 92.* FACILITIES: 79 sites, 30 ft. max RV length, 79 no hookups, tenting available, flush toilets, tables, fire rings, grills, wood. RECREATION: river/stream fishing, hiking trails. Open all year. Facilities fully operational May 15 through Sep 30. Phone: (801) 785-3563.

UINTA NATIONAL FOREST (Timpooneke Campground)—*From jct US 89 & Hwy 74: Go 4 mi N on Hwy 74, then 10 mi E on Hwy 92, then 4 mi SE on Alpine Loop (follow signs).* FACILITIES: 32 sites, 32 no hookups, tenting available, pit toilets, tables, fire rings, wood. RECREATION: stream fishing, hiking trails. Open mid May through late Oct. Phone: (801) 785-3563.

ANTIMONY—E-3

Otter Creek Marina & RV Park—An RV PARK and marina on a lake with a mountain view. *From jct Hwy 62 & Hwy 22: Go 4/10 mi E on Hwy 22.* ◇◇FACILITIES: 33 sites, 33 full hookups, (20 & 30 amp receptacles), 21 pull-thrus, tenting available, flush toilets, hot showers, sewage disposal, laundry, public phone, grocery store, ice, tables. ◇◇RECREATION: lake swimming, boating, 7 motor boat rentals, lake/river fishing. Open Mar 1 through Nov 1. Rate in 1993 $12 per vehicle. Phone: (800) 441-3292.

OTTER CREEK STATE PARK—*From town: Go 5 mi N on Hwy 22.* FACILITIES: 30 sites, 30 no hookups, flush toilets, hot showers, handicap restroom facilities, sewage disposal, grocery store, ice, tables, fire rings, grills, wood. RECREATION: lake swimming, boating, ramp, dock, lake fishing. Recreation open to the public. Open all year. Phone: (801) 624-3268.

BEAVER—E-2

► **BEAVER CANYON CAMPGROUND/MARIA'S COCINA**—*From jct I-15 (exit 112) & Business I-15: Go 1 mi S on Business I-15, then 1 1/2 mi E on Hwy 153.* Authentic Mexican food, 4 to 9 p.m. daily. Open May 1 through Nov 1. Master Card/Visa accepted. Phone: (801) 438-5654. FCRV 10% discount.
SEE AD THIS PAGE

BEAVER CANYON CAMPGROUND/MARIA'S COCINA—A rustic setting with a mountain view. Altitude 6000 ft. *From jct I-15 (exit 112) & Business I-15: Go 1 mi S on Business I-15, then 1 1/4 mi E on Hwy 153.* ◇◇◇FACILITIES: 105 sites, 31 full hookups, 26 water & elec (20 amp receptacles), 48 no hookups, seasonal sites, 55 pull-thrus, a/c allowed, phone hookups, tenting available, flush toilets, hot showers, laundry, public phone, limited grocery store, ice, tables, patios, fire rings, grills, wood. ◇RECREATION: pavilion, basketball hoop, playground.
Open Apr 15 through Nov 10. Rate in 1993 $10 for 2 persons. Master Card/Visa accepted. Phone: (801) 438-5654. FCRV 10% discount.
SEE AD THIS PAGE

DeLano Motel & RV Park—RV SPACES next to a motel in town. *From jct I-15 (exit 109) & Business Loop I-15: Go 2 mi E on Business Loop I-15.* FACILITIES: 12 sites, 12 full hookups, (20 amp receptacles), tenting available, flush toilets, hot showers, laundry, ice. Open all year. Rate in 1993 $8.50 for 2 persons. Phone: (801) 438-2418.

KOA-Beaver—A CAMPGROUND with shade near major highway with mountain view. *S'bound: From I-15 (exit 112): Go 3/4 mi E & S (left), then 1/4 mi (left) on Manderfield Rd. N'bound: From jct I-15 & Beaver/Manderfield (exit 112): Go 3/4 mi E & S (right), then 1/4 mi (left) on Manderfield Rd.* ◇◇◇FACILITIES: 75 sites, 25 full hookups, 41 water & elec (15,20 & 30 amp receptacles), 9 no hookups, 75 pull-thrus, tenting available, flush toilets, hot showers, sewage disposal, laundry, public phone, grocery store, LP gas refill by meter, ice, tables, grills. ◇◇RECREATION: rec room, swim pool, playground. Open Feb 1 through Nov 15. Rate in 1993 $15 for 2 persons. Phone: (801) 438-2924. KOA 10% value card discount.

MINERSVILLE STATE PARK—*From jct I-15 & Hwy 21: Go 11 mi W on Hwy 21.* FACILITIES: 29 sites, 11 water & elec, 18 no hookups, flush toilets, sewage disposal, tables. RECREATION: swimming, boating, ramp, dock, lake fishing. Open all year. Facilities fully operational May 1 through Nov 1.

United Beaver Camperland—A CAMPGROUND with a mountain view near major highway. *From I-15 (exit 109): Go 1 block E, then 1 block S on campground road.* ◇◇◇FACILITIES: 150 sites, 80 full hookups, 40 water & elec (20,30 & 50 amp receptacles), 30 no hookups, seasonal sites, 100 pull-thrus, tenting available, flush toilets, hot showers, laundry, public phone, grocery store, LP gas refill by meter, ice, tables, fire rings, grills. ◇◇RECREATION: rec room, swim pool, playground, horseshoes, volleyball. Open all year. Rate in 1993 $9.95-12.95 for 2 persons. Phone: (801) 438-2808.

BLANDING—E-5

Halls Crossing (Not Visited)—*From jct US 163/191 & Hwy 95: Go 38 mi W on Hwy 95, then 46 mi SW on US 163/276.* FACILITIES: 60 sites, 60 no hookups, flush toilets, cold showers, sewage disposal, laun-

BLANDING—Cont... HALLS CROSSING...
dry, tables, grills...
motor boat renta...
available upon re...

KAMPARK
and...
jct H...
191...
◇◇...
ups,...
no hookups, se...
lowed, heater al...
able, group site...
toilets, hot shov...
store, RV suppli...
RECREATION: ...
No pets. Open ...
persons. Americ...
Visa accepted.
SEE AD THIS ...

MANTI-LASA...
Campground)—*F...*
CILITIES: 30 sites...
chemical toilets, ...
Open May 15 thre...

HOVENWEER...
Ruin)—*From jct U...*
on Hwy 262 to Ha...
on dirt road. FA...
toilets, tables, fire...
Open all year.

❀ BOUNTIFUL...
320...
then...
on M...
char...
sells...
Open all year. D...
Phone: (801) 2...
SEE AD TRAVE...

BR...
GOLDEN ...
RATE...
rural...
91:...
FACI...
wate...
cles), 38 pull-t...
tenting available...
restroom faciliti...
grocery store, L...
RECREATION: p...
Open all year. Ra...
SEE AD THIS ...

KOA-Brigha...
setting with shade...
jct I-15 (exit 364...
3 1/2 mi S on U...
360) & Hwy 8...
◇◇FACILITIES:...
elec (20 & 30 a...
pull-thrus, tenting...

KO...

BEAVER...
1419 E...
P...

Ma...
"An Au...

Figure 5-3. *Both public and private campgrounds are included on this sample page from* Woodall's Campground Directory. *(Courtesy Woodall Publishing Company)*

Other information includes a brief description of the surroundings, altitude of the campground where pertinent, pet and reservation policies, and the credit cards accepted. Additionally, the *Trailer Life Directory* includes a description of the access road; average site width; maximum length of stay; extra charges for using an electric heater, air conditioner, and the cable TV hookup; and whether units with slide-outs can be accommodated (the sites in many older campgrounds are too narrow or close together for a slideout to be extended).

Both directories rate the campgrounds according to the facilities offered and cleanliness. *Woodall's* also rates recreational facilities and *Trailer Life* rates visual appeal and environmental quality of the campground.

Military campgrounds are listed separately in both directories. Only active and retired military personnel and their families can use these campgrounds; proper identification is required.

No directory, no matter how large, lists every campground, and each differs somewhat in what is listed. The big directories focus more on private campgrounds than public campgrounds; in some areas, only a few of many public campgrounds may be listed. (The reason for this, as you may have guessed, is because private campgrounds advertise in the directory and public campgrounds do not.)

AAA has regional campground directories that are free to members. These directories list only AAA-approved campgrounds and they are considerably smaller than other directories. The information about each campground, while not as detailed as that in other directories, contains the most essential information. AAA directories list many public campgrounds, especially those in national forests.

The largest national campground chain, Kampgrounds of America (KOA), publishes its own directory. It is free at any KOA campground or can be ordered from KOA, P.O. Box 30162, Billings, Montana 59107 (enclose $3 for shipping and handling on mail orders). A KOA Value Kard, available for $8, is good for two years and entitles the holder to a 10-percent discount at any KOA campground.

A directory of Yogi Bear's Jellystone Park Campground Resorts, another national chain with recreational facilities geared toward children, can be ordered by calling 1-800-558-2954.

Some type of campground directory should be used for trip planning. Don't rely on finding a campground from the highway signs with

Figure 5-4. *Highway signs with these icons indicate a campground. On main highways, underneath the icon sign is an arrow pointing in the direction of the campground. Don't rely solely on these signs when you are looking for a campground; use them in conjunction with a campground directory.*

a tent or trailer icon and a directional arrow (Figure 5-4). You don't know what type of campground awaits you or the distance to it, which could be as much as 5 miles away (the maximum distance a campground can be from such signs). Furthermore, if the sign has only the tent icon, the campground may not be suitable for RVs.

Campground Rates

When planning a trip, you will need to know what it costs to stay at campgrounds. Campground rates are considerably lower than those for motels but should be figured into the travel budget nonetheless.

Because of the time delay inherent in the publication process, rates listed in the *Trailer Life* and *Woodall's* directories are for the year prior to the publication date. Many current rates will be higher, but some will be the same. The smaller AAA directories list rates that are somewhat more current, and some are guaranteed, which means that the published rate won't change for the year in which the directory is current.

Even year-old rates can be used to compare all campgrounds in an area; the campgrounds with the highest or lowest fees last year will probably maintain the same general rate structure in the current year.

The fee for staying in a campground depends on which part of the country it's in, the facilities offered, occasionally the whim of the owner, and sometimes the rate is set to be in line with what is charged by other campgrounds in an area. Generally, campgrounds in and around large cities cost the most, one reason being that taxes and the cost of doing business are higher than in rural areas.

Rates of some resort campgrounds are often equal to those of metropolitan-area campgrounds. True resort campgrounds are typically built on expensive land in highly desirable vacation areas and have all types of recreational facilities: certainly a swimming pool, maybe tennis courts, perhaps even an 18-hole golf course (Figure 5-5). Rates are set so the owner can pay off the debt for acquiring and developing the property and maintaining the campground and facilities.

Next lower on the rate scale are campgrounds near towns and cities on an interstate highway. RVers usually pay more for the convenience of the "easy off, easy on" access to the interstate. Of course, any campground so located will be noisy from the traffic. One campground we know of offers a lower rate for the sites nearest the highway.

Campgrounds in national forests and parks and on BLM lands generally have the lowest rates. None of these campgrounds have hookups, so the rates vary in accordance with the level of development (i.e., flush or pit toilets, drinking water, and a dump station). Showers are almost

Figure 5-5. *Pacific Shores RV Park, Newport, Oregon, is a resort campground that offers an indoor heated pool, among other amenities.*

nonexistent in these campgrounds. No fee is charged at many out-of-the-way or little-used forest service and BLM campgrounds.

Rates at Corps of Engineers (COE) campgrounds tend to be slightly higher than those operated by other federal agencies. COE campgrounds are always on a body of water and often have sites with some or all hookups. The less developed COE campgrounds have lower rates.

Low rates are often found in campgrounds in municipal parks of some small towns, especially those located on secondary highways. The campground may have electric and water hookups at each site, flush toilets and showers in the washroom, and a dump station, yet still have a very low rate. Some are free, but when there is no charge, hookups are rare; however, flush toilets and showers may be available.

It used to be that you could count on state parks to have reasonable rates; some still do, but the rates at many are fast approaching those of mid-priced private campgrounds, yet often the hookups are not on a par with those in private campgrounds. In some state parks, residents and non-residents pay the same fee, but in others, non-residents pay more.

Although the rate for campsites in some state parks is reasonable, an additional daily use fee may be charged (every year we find more parks imposing this fee). The use fee must be paid every day, whether or not you leave the park. The daily charge varies from state to state, and ranges from 50 cents to $6. Annual passes are available and are worthwhile for RVers who use the park frequently or who stay for a week or two.

Campground rates in state recreation areas are sometimes slightly lower than in more fully developed state park campgrounds.

Between campgrounds with the highest and lowest rates is a broad segment of private campgrounds with rates as varied as the campgrounds. Some have a flat rate that includes all hookups; others have a base rate with an additional fee for all hookups or a separate fee for each hookup. With each hookup priced separately, a full hookup site typically is $3 to $5 more than the base rate.

As may be expected, recently built campgrounds have rates on the higher side. Campgrounds located on highways that were bypassed when an interstate was built often have lower than average rates.

Private campground rates range upward from $10, but numerous public campgrounds have rates under $10. Private campground rates, on the high side, are $25 to $30.

Some campgrounds have coin-operated showers—a quarter buys enough water for a rather spartan shower.

Electricity may be metered at each site. Paying the amount for electricity actually consumed usually applies to RVers staying a week or longer, but we once stayed overnight in a campground and paid the metered rate. If you occupy a site, there is often no charge for using the campground dump station, but sometimes it does cost extra.

An extra charge may be imposed for using an electric heater, air conditioner, the cable TV hookup, and a telephone hookup at the site (telephone service is offered at some campgrounds).

The base rate is usually for a specific number of people occupying the RV, with an extra charge imposed for each additional person. The rate allows for a motorhome and dinghy or trailer and tow vehicle to be parked in the site; more vehicles may cost more. There may be an extra charge for pets as well. Be aware that pets aren't allowed in some campgrounds.

We once received a discount that amounted to more than 20 percent of the normal rate because we didn't use the campground's washroom (we wish this were the policy in more campgrounds).

In some localities, the bed tax on motel and hotel rooms also applies to campground sites. No matter what the name of a local tax, it increases the rate, sometimes considerably. Local taxes are not reflected in rates in campground directories.

Campground rates for extended stays are usually lower than if the daily rate were paid for the stay. A common weekly rate arrangement is to pay for six days and receive the seventh day free.

Free Camping in Campgrounds and Non-Campgrounds

Because an RV affords household conveniences without external connections, some people envision RVing as a vagabonding lifestyle and think they can simply pull off the road and camp wherever they take the notion. This freedom is appealing to us too, and, in our travels, if we happen to find an attractive place to camp that happens to be free, we often stop for a day or so. Some RVers, however, will go out of their way just to avoid paying for a camping spot. We met one RVer who boasted about how many nights he had been able to camp free, but some of the places he stayed weren't legitimate camping areas. We enjoy free camping—it's certainly easy on the pocketbook—but we don't go out of our way to avoid paying a fee. Any free camping we do has to be where we want to camp and where camping is allowed.

Legitimate places to camp free are decreasing, but plenty still exist with this attractive rate. If a campground is free, it will be a public campground—one administered by either federal, state, county, or city government or a local civic organization. Lions Clubs in some communities have established public campgrounds, many of which are free.

Most free campgrounds are in the western states, which is understandable because they aren't as heavily populated as the eastern states. There are also more federal lands in the West, and camping is allowed on many of these lands whether or not there are designated campgrounds.

Although free campgrounds may be found in town or county parks, state forests and recreation areas, and national wildlife areas, most are in national forests. Where there is no charge, the camping is usually primitive, but pit toilets, a central water supply, and a dump station may be available.

In the West, many free, federally administered campgrounds are 20 to 30 miles from a main highway, and the access road is usually gravel or dirt. Many of these roads cannot be safely negotiated with even mid-size RVs, let alone large ones.

Free camping is sometimes available in other than a designated campground. Many times we have enjoyed free camping in open meadows and along rivers and streams on national forest lands, in some state fishing access areas, and in wide parking areas adjacent to a road that runs through public lands. We never camp in such places if a no-camping notice is posted, and we never camp on private land unless invited to do so by the owner.

Free municipal campgrounds are found only in small towns. It's difficult to camp free in large urban areas. If you could find a place to park your rig without violating local ordinances, it may be unsafe; since you aren't in a designated campground, the security afforded by other RVers is nonexistent. If you camp anyway, hope the local police patrol the area where you are parked. If they do, however, they may run you out.

The large parking lots of supermarkets and shopping centers may seem to be obvious choices for free urban overnighting, but overnight RV parking is prohibited in many. If no restrictions are posted, you may be able to obtain permission to park from one of the complex's store managers. Prohibitions on overnighting in parking lots are common in places that have several private campgrounds to service RVers.

You may be allowed to stay overnight in a restaurant parking lot if you eat there. How "free" this is depends on the price of the meal. It's not a good practice to stay in a parking lot if you don't patronize the business.

It used to be that you could count on spending a free, albeit noisy, night at truckstops, but at some we recently have found charges being imposed for overnighting. If there is a charge, you may be assigned a place to park where you can have an electric hookup; we hesitate to call these places "sites" because most of them aren't.

Rather than allowing you to park your RV in the truckstop, you may be directed to an adjacent campground, often under the same ownership. Parking there will not be free, of course. Since many truckstops are on interstate highways, an adjacent campground is likely to have the usual higher rates. There are still some truckstops where you can park free, however, and in some service stations with spacious parking areas, you may be allowed to stay free if you refuel there, but get permission from the manager beforehand.

Highway rest areas with spacious parking areas, picnic facilities, and restrooms would seem logical and convenient spots for free overnighting; however, each state has different rules—some lenient, some not—regarding rest area RV parking. It is prohibited in many states and strictly regulated where it is allowed. Parking of any vehicle may be limited to a few hours, although some states have an 18-hour limit, which obviously means that staying overnight is permissible. Pay attention to the limits to avoid being routed out by the highway patrol.

Rules are constantly changing regarding overnighting in highway rest areas, and you can be sure that when changed, they become more restrictive. (See Chapter 9 for more about camping in highway rest areas.)

Vacationing RVers may be invited by their friends to park in their driveways. If you intend to do this, either overnight as you pass through or for a longer period, be sure that local ordinances allow it. Many communities, mostly in large cities and their suburbs, prohibit parking RVs on streets and driveways, and in yards as well. Small towns and

Figure 5-6. *A Coast-to-Coast affiliate, Whalers Rest RV Resort, South Beach, Oregon, is an example of a nicely landscaped and well laid out membership campground.*

rural areas aren't likely to have these restrictions.

The *American PC United States Public Campgrounds Recreational Vehicle Directory* lists more than 6,800 free and low-fee campgrounds. It is available from American PC Campground Directory, P.O. Box 820009, Dallas, Texas 75382; 214-987-3440.

Membership Campgrounds

Membership campgrounds are a fairly recent development on the RVing scene (Figure 5-6). Whether joining a campground association is practical for you depends on your RVing lifestyle, where and how often you travel, and your budget.

In certain respects, belonging to a membership campground can be compared to having a timeshare in a resort condominium. Membership entitles the holder to stay for a specific period each year at the campground where the member joins—known as the "home campground." Unlike a timeshare that restricts you to one place for one period, a campground membership allows members to stay at any of the association campgrounds whenever they want; the length of any one stay is usually restricted, however.

A typical membership costs thousands of dollars; on the high side,

---

Table 5-1. Annual Camping Costs*
of Membership Campground

$5,000 (initial dues) amortized over 10 years	$500 per year
Dues	$200 per year
Total costs	$700 per year
Camping for 33 days ($700 divided by 33)	$21.21 per day

Note:
  *Actual annual costs could be higher or lower than those shown.

---

it could cost as much as $10,000. The initial cost does not have to be paid all at once; it can be financed. In addition, annual dues are in the $200-to-$300 range. Stays at the home campground are free, but some associations charge $1 or $2 for each overnight stay at affiliate campgrounds.

Amortization of membership campground costs may be estimated as follows: Let's say your membership costs $5,000 and you will be paying it off for 10 years. Amortized, the cost is $500 a year. Adding $200 for dues brings the annual expenditure to $700. If each year you spend a three-week vacation and six weekends (33 days) in your home

---

Table 5-2. Annual Camping Costs*
of Membership Campground

$10,000 (initial dues) amortized over 10 years	$1,000 per year
Dues	$200 per year
Total costs	$1,200 per year
Camping for 33 days ($1,200 divided by 33)	$36.36 per day

Note:
  *Actual annual costs could be higher or lower than those shown.

Table 5-3. Annual Camping Costs* with Stays at Membership Campgrounds

$5,000 (initial dues) amortized over 10 years	$500 per year
Dues	$200 per year
Fixed costs	$700 per year
Camping at affiliated campgrounds ($2 x 14 days)	$28
Camping at home campground (16 days)	No charge
Total costs	$728 per year
Camping for 30 days (14 + 16) ($728 ÷ 30)	$24.27 per day

Note:
　*Actual annual costs could be higher or lower than those shown.

campground, you will pay $21.21 each day. Using the same example but with a $10,000 membership cost, each day will cost $36.36. Another example: With a $5,000 membership and $200 annual dues, if you spend eight weekends a year at your home campground and two weeks at other affiliated campgrounds, paying $2 a day, each day averages out to $24.27 (see Tables 5-1, 5-2, and 5-3).

Because finance charges, miscellaneous costs, and assessments are not included in these examples, the per-day costs are not accurate; they will be higher than shown. The examples illustrate how to roughly determine whether joining a membership campground is cost-effective for you.

Other factors that should be considered include the following:

• Is the home campground close enough to be used on weekends?

• Are the limits on the length of stay in the home campground acceptable? (Depending on the campground, the limits can range from 14 to 30 days.)

• Does it make a difference if the home campground is open all year or is strictly seasonal?

• Are other campgrounds in the association located where you expect to travel?

The three largest membership campground associations are Coast-to-Coast Resorts, whose campgrounds are independently owned affiliates, and Thousand Trails and its sister group NACO, both of which own a large percentage of their campgrounds. Each association has campgrounds all over the country. While there are many close together in popular vacation areas, they may be few and far between in other locations.

You can obtain the names of nearby Coast-to-Coast campgrounds (where you can join the association) from Coast-to-Coast Resorts, 64 Inverness Drive East, Englewood, Colorado 80112; 303-790-2267. Literature and a directory of campgrounds in your area are offered by Thousand Trails and NACO; the address for both is: 12301 N.E. 10th Place, Bellevue, Washington 98005; 206-455-3155.

A number of smaller membership campground associations exist; they don't have as many campgrounds as the three largest, but the cost of membership is considerably lower—sometimes under $1,000. Some of the smaller associations advertise in RVing publications and have brochures available where RVers are likely to see them.

After you purchase an RV, you may be contacted by a membership campground in your vicinity. Some membership campground associations have booths at RV shows. When certain brands of RVs are purchased, new owners may receive a complimentary short-term membership.

A campground brochure that advertises one or two nights of free camping is almost certainly from a membership campground. On the brochure is stipulated that the free night(s) applies only if the guest attends a sales presentation during the stay. If the length of time for the presentation is not mentioned, figure on about an hour.

When buying a campground membership:

• Read and understand everything in the contract before signing it.

• Ask as many questions as necessary for clarification.

• Understand that if you and your spouse purchase a lifetime membership and one of you dies, the other is responsible for fulfilling the contract obligations until he or she dies.

• Carefully weigh any propositions.

• Don't be rushed into a decision; some salespeople may try to high-pressure you into signing.

• Come to the sales presentation armed with a calculator to break down the costs (using our examples as a guide).

Trip Information

Only you know where you want to go on an RVing trip, but you may want some help in the actual planning. You can select the route yourself, or have it laid out for you if you belong to an auto club that provides this service. The packets from state tourism offices and trip guides from auto clubs are useful.

AAA TourBooks are very complete, listing sightseeing attractions with locations, hours, and admission prices. In addition, the entries for large cities describe the best routes for driving in and around the city and where shopping areas are located. National parks, monuments, forests, and recreation areas have detailed write-ups with valuable information for RVers, including roads that are unsuitable for trailers or large motorhomes. Consulting the book for Glacier National Park, for instance, you will find that a portion of Going-to-the-Sun Road, the only route through the park, is restricted from mid-June to mid-September to vehicle combinations no longer than 24 feet or wider than 8 feet. In Olympic National Park, you would know which unpaved roads in the park are not suitable for RVs.

The same information can also be found in some state literature and on some maps. Watch for any roads on your intended route marked "Closed in winter"; these are always high-altitude routes through mountains. Depending on the severity of the previous winter, they may not open until late June.

Some travelers on time-limited vacations try to go too far in too short a time. Your trips will be more enjoyable and relaxing if you plan an easy schedule, keeping the day's runs short enough to allow frequent stops for breaks from traveling and for sightseeing.

If you have returned from a vacation worn out from the trip, chances are it is because you drove several hundred miles every day and perhaps were under pressure to arrive on time because of advance reservations. Avoid vacations that seem more like work than play by planning trips with an end destination closer to home—or even better, with no fixed destination at all. This enables you to have short driving days, and each day's run can be tailored to suit your mood. If you feel like driving just 50 miles or you want to stay put, you can do either without upsetting any plans.

One of the greatest advantages of driving short distances, no more than 200 miles, is that it is not tiring. Also arriving at campgrounds early in the day, before they begin to fill up, makes advance reservations (at most campgrounds) unnecessary. With an early arrival, the afternoon is free for sightseeing, shopping, or relaxing at the campground's pool. When traveling with small children, keep daily runs short, or at least stop often to let the kids get out and burn off some energy.

Another benefit of short runs is that you won't be driving or arriving after dark. It's difficult to maneuver into a site and set up camp in the dark; it's a real chore when you are tired from driving all day.

Short daily runs allow you to sleep late when vacationing, if you wish. You can leave at the campground's check-out time, whether it's eleven o'clock, noon, or later; we have had several one o'clock departures after spending the morning sightseeing or relaxing. It is often possible to stay after the official check-out time if you clear this with the campground manager.

With no set destination, you can spend as much time as your vacation allows going anywhere that takes your fancy. You can stop at places along the way and spend some time there instead of hurrying on.

Most people's jobs are structured with regular tasks and scheduled appointments. To really benefit from a vacation, change your routine entirely by not saddling yourself with routines and schedules. Roam free and unfettered for a time, getting as far away as you can from our structured, hectic, fast-paced society; it's marvelously refreshing and relaxing.

A leisurely vacation is certainly more relaxing for you, but also benefits your rig. Frequent stops allow the tires and the motorhome or tow vehicle engine to cool down, which is beneficial; on a tight schedule, few RVers stop more often than is necessary. The more miles driven, the more bumps and curves encountered—each affecting items stored in the cabinets. The disarray caused by items shifting, falling, or breaking increases proportionately with length of time spent driving.

If you must travel on a tight schedule, allow some leeway for the unexpected possibilities: bad weather, rig breakdowns, and highway construction delays.

Selecting a Campground

With a campground directory, you can preselect your campgrounds or select them as you go. Sometimes, after we set out from a campground, we have no idea of where we will stay that night. We enjoy this type of traveling, being free to stop at a place that appeals to us, but some people prefer to know exactly where they are going.

Whichever way you travel, be sure to check the campground directory for pertinent information other than the general amenities you want. You may prefer a pull-through rather than a back-in site, or you may need a campground where pets are allowed. It is important to note whether the campground is actually in the town under which it is listed, or if the town is the nearest point of reference. In sparsely settled states, some campgrounds are as far as 85 miles from the listed town; sometimes 10 or 15 miles from town may be too far away for your purposes. Campgrounds at a distance from town may have lower rates than those in town, but consider your trips for shopping and refueling before assuming that staying out of town is a bargain.

If you plan to stay in a campground in a national forest, pay particular attention to the RV length the sites can accommodate. Many national forest campgrounds have length limits of 22 or 16 feet. (Some private campgrounds have length limits as well; typically, RVs longer than 35 feet can't be accommodated.) We habitually scout out national forest campgrounds in our truck without the trailer, and usually find one or two sites that longer RVs can fit into. The access roads, however, are often unsuited for large RVs: The curves are too tight and the trees are too close to the road, so there is no place to swing wide enough to get around the curve. Another problem: There is no way of knowing in advance if the larger sites are occupied.

Most private campgrounds have no limit on the length of stay, but a one- or two-week limit is common in public campgrounds. If you intend to stay a week or a month at a private campground, find out if lower rates are offered.

Reservations

If you will be traveling in peak tourist seasons in popular vacation areas, it is wise to make reservations for stays of longer than overnight. The more popular the area, the earlier the reservation should be made. At some campgrounds, weekends are booked far in advance.

If you habitually drive until late in the day, a reservation is a good idea. We try to make our runs short in order to arrive early, but if we find ourselves still on the road in late afternoon, we call ahead to make a reservation—in most cases, a space will be held until 6:00 P.M. without a deposit. Reservations are always advised at membership campgrounds, even if you are just staying overnight.

Reservations are not taken in many national parks, but in some they are recommended. All national park reservations are made through MISTIX Consumer Services (1-800-365-2267). Sites in some national forest campgrounds can be reserved through the Forest Service Reservation Center (1-800-280-2267). A reservation fee is charged for both, in addition to the campsite fee. Payment in advance, by check or credit card, is also required.

Understand the reservation policy before you reserve a site. A deposit may be required; in case your plans change, you should know how much of the deposit, if any, will be refunded.

Ready Cash During Travel

RVers are sometimes perplexed about how to keep ready cash available during travel. This should not be a cause for concern because nowadays cash can be obtained, country-wide, so the need to carry large amounts of money is eliminated.

Traveler's checks are a safe way to carry large amounts of cash, especially for foreign travel, but they may not be the most practical for traveling in the United States. Traveler's checks are supposed to be universally recognized as cash, but we have experienced difficulty using them as cash. We have encountered store clerks who think traveler's checks are a type of personal check and won't accept them; store managers will usually okay them, however.

We stopped using traveler's checks a long time ago for this reason, as well as to avoid paying a large amount up front and having it on our balance if we used a credit card to purchase the checks. It's now more convenient to obtain our money in smaller amounts, as we need it.

The best and least expensive method is to withdraw funds from your checking or savings account by using an automatic teller machine

(ATM). The identification card issued by a bank when you open an account will be imprinted with the logos of ATM systems at which it can be used. In addition to the bank's own ATMs, most cards can be used in ATMs with the Plus or Cirrus system (many ATMs throughout the country have both). When your card is issued, you will receive a Personal Identification Number (PIN), which is needed for all ATM transactions. Depending on the bank, PIN numbers are assigned or you can choose your own.

Using an ATM is simple. After inserting your card, follow the instructions that appear on the ATM's small, TV-like screen. A dollar may be deducted from your account for any transactions made at a bank other than your own or its branches. Storage space is limited in ATMs, so withdrawals are usually restricted to $200 from one card in each 24-hour period; if you need more, simply go to another ATM. Most ATMs can be used at any hour of the day or night. ATMs are also available at convenience stores, truckstops, and supermarkets.

A Visa or Mastercard can also be used to obtain cash from an ATM or from a bank teller. Credit card cash advances are expensive and should only be used in emergency situations. You are borrowing money from the credit card company; as with all loans, interest has to be paid. A finance charge is also common. If you can't pay the total amount of the bill when it is due, the cash costs you even more since the prevailing rate of credit card interest—always double-digit, usually in the 17- to 19-percent range—is added to all charges that are paid off in monthly installments.

A green, gold, or platinum American Express card can be used to obtain cash at selected ATMs. You must have an American Express PIN and you must provide American Express with the name of a designated bank in which you have an account. The amount withdrawn from the ATM, and a small service fee, will be deducted automatically from your bank account.

Take reasonable safety precautions when using an ATM. Don't allow anyone to peer over your shoulder when entering your PIN. Be aware of bystanders around an ATM; watch their actions. Many robbers stake out ATMs; people leaving will probably have money, making them a desirable target. It's best to use ATMs during daylight hours; if you must use one after dark, be aware of cars parked near the machine—some thieves like to wait in comfort for their next victim.

Most campground fees can be paid with personal checks, but don't count on using them for fuel, restaurant meals, and other travel purchases, unless the check is drawn on a local bank. If your bank has branches in several states, a personal check can sometimes be used to obtain cash away from home. You can write a personal check for cash, up to a designated limit, at any branch, and the funds will be withdrawn from your account at home. If you often travel out of state, it is advantageous to have an account in a multistate bank.

 *Chapter 6*

Readying an RV for Travel

Certain preparations are necessary before you set off on an RVing trip: All supplies and equipment must be securely stowed with weight distribution in mind, and the rig itself must be checked. This chapter will help you with these preparations.

Food and Related Items

Most people enjoy eating out on vacation; if you are among them, keep this in mind when provisioning your RV. It's a common tendency of RVers to take along too much food; storage space is taken up needlessly and the extra weight of unused food is hauled both going and coming.

The quantity of food taken depends on the route you travel and what your destination is. If towns are on your route, food shopping can be done as needed; it's not necessary to load enough for the entire trip before setting out. Grocery shopping can be interesting and educational because you will find regional foods and brands unavailable at home. On the other hand, if you are heading into sparsely settled country, you have no choice but to take along everything you will need.

Paper plates and plastic flatware are suitable for some foods, and using them cuts down on clean-up chores, but unbreakable dinnerware and metal flatware also should be taken. If you purchase special sets to be kept in the RV, you won't need to pack them for every trip. Take only the utensils regularly used at home and a limited number of pots and skillets; a large amount of food can't be cooked in a small container, but a small amount can always be cooked in a large one. Because most cooking appliances are bulky, you should take only those you use most frequently, such as a toaster and a coffeemaker.

Clothing and Linens

In addition to personal grooming items, each person should bring along a variety of clothing—everyday wear and special-purpose clothing such as swimwear—as befits the season and vacation locale. If there isn't enough storage space to keep a supply of clean clothes for the entire trip, laundry can be done as needed because many campgrounds and even the smallest towns have self-service laundries.

The linen supply should include what is needed for the galley (dish towels and potholders), the bath (hand and bath towels and washcloths), and beds (sheets, pillowcases, blankets, and/or sleeping bags).

Other Equipment

You will need something to clean the floor; it's bound to get dirty often. A hand vacuum is useful for carpeting. For vinyl floor coverings, a whisk broom does the job as well as a vacuum. Most carpet sweepers are too large to be conveniently used in RVs, but small models are available at RV supply stores.

If the RV has a generator, or electric hookups will be available, a small electric fan may be useful, even if the RV is equipped with an air conditioner; for cool climes, you may want an electric heater to take the chill off.

If children are along, be sure to include puzzles, games, and books, in addition to toys, to keep them occupied on rainy days.

A small tool kit is handy. It should include (at least) pliers, hammer, crescent wrench, utility or pocket knife, duct tape, and screwdrivers with different tips (including a square tip, which fits the type of screw commonly used in RV construction) or one screwdriver with changeable tips, and screws in various sizes. A hand drill and an assortment of bits are also useful. We often use large slip-joint pliers to remove the cap from a sewer drain. These tools are in addition to the automotive tools, such as jacks and lug wrenches.

Unless you really want to get away from it all, you may take along a TV or a portable stereo. Some people purchase a small TV that runs on either AC or DC, so they can use it with or without an electric hookup.

Make a permanent checklist of everything that needs to be loaded into the RV and keep it for future trips. List only those items taken from home, not anything that is normally kept in the RV between trips. The following basic list can be used as a guide; it includes a few obvious items that are often overlooked. Your own list should be considerably more detailed and adjusted according to your individual needs.

Food

Seasonings, spices (including salt and pepper)

Sugar

Dinnerware, flatware

Can opener

Cooking utensils, knives

Pots, skillets

Appliances

Recipes

Toothpicks

Paper towels, napkins

Foil, plastic wrap, plastic bags

Dishwashing liquid

Charcoal, lighter fluid

Toilet paper

Clothing

Sewing kit

Personal grooming items

Linens for bath, bed, galley

Vacuum, broom and dustpan, or small carpet sweeper

Electric fan

Electric heater

TV

Portable stereo

Toys, puzzles, games, books

Writing supplies (paper, pens)

Tool kit

Flashlight

Extra batteries for all battery-operated equipment

First-aid kit

Medications

Warranties for the RV and its equipment should always be kept in the RV. If you have a problem on the road, a warranty won't do you any good if it's at home. For ease in locating warranties, keep them together in a large envelope, or two-pocket portfolio as we do. Don't use a file folder because papers can fall out.

On our checklist, each entry has a row of boxes after it so it can be

Figure 6-1. *Paper towels fill empty space in a cabinet, keeping things in place during travel.*

used for many trips. (When a list is filled up, we make a photocopy of our master list.)

Storage

Stow breakable items and containers so they will travel safely. Put heavy items where they can't slide, shift, or chafe against anything. Free-standing living room chairs with a wide base may travel safely in an upright position, but most freestanding dining tables need to be turned over and the chairs laid down; otherwise, they will topple over when the RV is in motion. (Some RV manufacturers provide fasteners for securing freestanding dining sets.)

Items stored in cabinets can "walk" from vibration and slide when the RV turns corners, so cabinets should be lined with a non-skid material (available by the foot at RV supply stores) and packed to eliminate empty space. Rolls of paper towels make excellent space fillers for cabinets; they are lightweight and provide cushioning (Figure 6-1). Rolled fabric towels or clothing can be used for the same purpose in cabinets where non-food breakable items, such as a stereo or camera, are stored.

Small items that are stored in the cabinet under the galley sink and in other large cabinets can be put in boxes to ensure they will travel safely. In our under-sink cabinet, we have a large square plastic box in which we keep bottles of cooking oil, vinegar, syrup, and other liquids that would make a mess if they broke or spilled. The box is packed with enough containers so that there is no room for anything to fall over (Figure 6-2).

We also use boxes to fill space in other cabinets and outside compartments so nothing can shift, and to provide compartmentalized storage for small items. If they are contained, small items aren't likely to become lost.

When loading the RV, store heavy items in low cabinets or on the floor, but don't put them on plumbing pipes or electrical wires, or where they could slide into the water pump or other fixed equipment.

Store only lightweight items in overhead cabinets; where breakable items are stored, be sure the cabinet doors latch securely.

All but the most lightweight items stored on a bed, chair, or sofa during travel are likely to bounce off.

Pack the refrigerator so nothing can spill or break. Use breadstuffs and

Figure 6-2. *Foods that would make a mess if spilled during travel can be stored in a box so they won't fall over or break. At top right is a portion of a shelf installed on the sink's drainpipe. It's just the right size for storing boxes of foil, plastic wrap, waxed paper, and plastic bags.*

soft drink cans for refrigerator fillers, but remember that space for air circulation is needed for proper cooling. If the refrigerator has been tightly packed for traveling, remove some of the items before turning it on.

The refrigerator should be precooled before storing perishables in it. It's best to allow it to cool overnight before the next day's departure. If this can't be done, allow a minimum of two hours for cooling. Only cold foods should be put in the refrigerator. Because much of the cold is lost when loading the refrigerator, keep loading time to a minimum. When finished, keep the door shut so the refrigerator can recool while power is still available.

Some RVers with motorhomes, pickup campers, and vans equipped with two-way, 120-/12-volt, or three-way AES refrigerators operate them on 12 volts during travel, while some with two-way, 120-volt/ propane refrigerators operate them on propane. For safety reasons (see

Chapter 9), we keep our 120-volt/propane refrigerator turned off during travel. If the refrigerator is well filled with cold items and we don't open the door or drive for more than five hours (a normal long day's run for us), the refrigerator stays cold, even in hot weather.

Before moving the RV, ensure that the refrigerator door is tightly shut; if the door is not self-locking, make sure that the door-securing device is in place.

Weight Distribution

If weight is distributed evenly throughout the RV, trailers are easier to tow, motorhomes handle better, and all parts of the suspension system carry equal weight. An RV that is obviously down in the rear or leaning to one side needs to have some cargo either shifted or removed.

The only exception to having weight distributed evenly is with some conventional trailers. If the hitch, or tongue, weight is too low, the trailer will fishtail at highway speeds. Hitch weights are listed in the manufacturer's brochure. If the weight falls below the percentages shown in Table 6-1, it needs to be increased by stowing enough weight in front of the axles. It may take some experimenting to get the right weight distribution. Too much hitch weight adversely affects the braking, cornering, and handling of the tow vehicle and may cause suspension and drive-train damage.

Table 6-1. Trailer Hitch (Tongue) Weight

Conventional Trailers	
Trailer Weight	Hitch (Tongue) Weight
Up to 2,000 lb.	No more than 200 lb.
More than 2,000 lb.	12–15 percent of trailer weight
Fifth-Wheel Trailers	
Trailer Weight	Hitch Weight
All weights	25 percent of trailer weight

If the water tank is in front of the axles, the hitch weight varies according to how much water is in the tank. You will learn how much, if any, to have in the tank when the trailer is in tow. (A tip: If weight distribution is not a factor, to avoid hauling the considerable weight of a full water tank, fill the tank with only enough water to satisfy your needs during travel, unless you are going where there won't be a water hookup.)

Another Checklist

In addition to stowing the items taken aboard for a trip, you'll have some other things to do before the RV is ready to go, including filling the water tank, propane cylinders, and fuel tank on the tow vehicle or motorhome, and making a check of the running gear. So nothing will be forgotten, make a checklist containing such items, and keep it where you can refer to it before every trip. The list may look like this:

Fill water tank to necessary level.

Fill propane cylinders.

Fill automotive fuel tank.

Check oil in engine.

Check windshield-washer fluid.

Fill generator fuel tank.

Check fluid level in wet-cell batteries.

Clean battery terminals.

Inflate tires to proper pressure.

Check wheel lugs for tightness.

Attach towing mirrors (if necessary).

Lubricate running gear (if necessary).

Test smoke detector.

Test carbon monoxide detector (if the RV is so equipped).

Be sure tires are inflated to the proper pressure (indicated on the sidewall) before taking your rig on the highway. This is especially important for RVers because a tire won't reach its maximum load-carrying capacity until inflated to the proper pressure. Moreover, under-inflation affects braking and handling (wandering and pulling to the right or left) and also contributes to increased fuel consumption and shortened tire life.

On the other hand, never overinflate tires. The heat that builds up as the tires are rolling, combined with the heavy weight they carry, can cause blowouts.

RVers should never take to the road unless the vehicle they drive is fitted with adequate mirrors. They should be large enough so that reflected images can be easily seen. Mirrors should have a convex section for wide and blind-spot viewing—the larger the better, because images appear smaller in convex mirrors than in flat mirrors. Some mirrors have a convex portion, or a separate convex mirror can be attached. Motorhomes usually have adequate mirrors, as do tow vehicles equipped with a towing package. If a vehicle doesn't come with suitable mirrors, you can purchase them from RV and automotive supply stores.

Before moving the rig, with a trailer straight behind the tow vehicle or an auxiliary vehicle in line with the motorhome, the driver should sit in the driver's seat and adjust the side mirrors for optimum road and rig visibility. Take the time to position them correctly before moving the rig. Have someone position the passenger-side mirror for you unless it can be automatically adjusted from the driver's seat. Just a slight adjustment may result in seeing a portion of the rig previously out of view. Properly adjusted side mirrors provide a view of the road behind, as well as the rear edge of the RV and trailer tires. The driver's-side mirror should have a view (somewhat limited, however) of the rear tires of a motorhome or tow vehicle. An auxiliary vehicle, being narrower than the motor-home towing it, cannot be seen in the mirrors.

Most RVers need to become accustomed to using only the side mirrors because, when towing a trailer, all that can be seen in the rearview mirror is the front of the trailer, and some motorhomes are too long for a rearview mirror to be useful; some may not even have a rear window. Some motorhomers use TV-camera monitoring systems, which are designed primarily for use when backing but are also useful for driving.

If the RV hasn't been moved for some time, the lubricant has probably settled to the bottom of the wheel bearings. When you start out, drive slowly for a few minutes to allow the lubricant to spread throughout the bearings.

Hitching

After all the loading, supplying, and checking, it's time for trailerists to hitch the unit to the tow vehicle. With a conventional trailer, perform the following steps after the ball mount is inserted and secured in the hitch receiver:

1. Using the tongue jack, raise the trailer tongue high enough to clear the ball.

2. Back the tow vehicle until the ball is under the coupler on the end of the tongue.

3. Using the tongue jack, lower the tongue onto the ball and latch the coupler.

Positioning the ball under the coupler in Step 2 causes the most problems. When we had a conventional trailer, we devised a simple method for this critical positioning: First, the driver backs the tow vehicle until it's about 2 feet from the coupler, in as straight a line with the trailer as possible. Another person, who directs the hitching operation, is stationed at the left side of the tongue. With the ball mount in the hitch receiver, the "director" envisions the ball mount as an arrow pointing straight back. If the arrow points to the left of the coupler, the director tells the driver to turn the wheels of the tow vehicle to the right; if the arrow points to the right, the wheels are turned to the left (Figure 6-3). After slightly turning the wheels in the proper direction, the driver slowly backs. During the backing, the imaginary arrow should move until it points at the coupler. When it does, the driver is signaled to stop. Next, the driver straightens the wheels and moves straight back until the ball is under the coupler.

This is hardly an exact science, so the maneuver may have to be repeated several times, even to the point of pulling forward and starting all over again. If so, it is important not to go too far forward because the greater the distance between the coupler and the ball, the more the alignment problem is compounded. The procedure becomes easier and more exact as the two people involved become familiar with it.

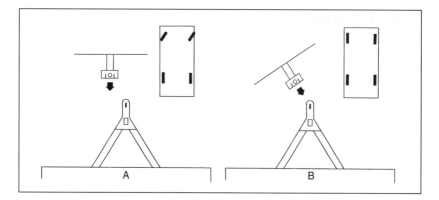

Figure 6-3. *With the ball mount and coupler positioned as shown in A, the wheels of the tow vehicle will have to be turned to the right in order to align the imaginary arrow with the coupler. As the tow vehicle backs, the imaginary arrow will move until it points at the coupler, as shown in B.*

Hitching a tow dolly to a motorhome or locating a tow bar can also be done using this procedure.

If the coupler won't latch, pull forward just a fraction of an inch. (If it won't unlatch when unhitching, back up a bit.) Slightly raising or lowering the tongue may aid in latching. Never assume the coupler is latched; always check it by raising the tongue with the jack. The rear of the tow vehicle will come up if the coupler is latched.

Trailerists with lightweight conventional units won't have a weight-distributing hitch (see the next paragraph), and all that remains for them to complete the hitching is crossing the safety chains under the hitch and hooking the ends in the chain loops (or holes) on the receiver. (On our conventional trailer, we replaced the hooks with screw-type quick links to prevent the safety chains from bouncing off the loops during travel.) Crossing the chains forms a cradle that (theoretically) catches the tongue and keeps it from dropping to the road if the trailer becomes disengaged, and also keeps the trailer from wandering too far from the tow vehicle's centerline.

On a weight-distributing hitch (Figure 6-4), a bracket incorporating the ball-mount and spring-bar receptacles is attached to the shank that fits into the hitch receiver. After the coupler is latched on the ball, the hitching procedure is more involved:

1. Insert the spring bars in the bracket receptacles.

2. Remove the safety pin from the chain-lift bracket and tip down the chain lift. (*Hint:* Place the safety pin on the tongue next to the bracket so it won't get lost in grass or gravel.)

3. Put the appropriate chain link over the hook on the chain lift.

4. Use the handle to raise the chain lift.

5. Replace the safety pin.

Raising the chain lift produces some resistance because tension is being put on the spring bars. Stand in front of the bracket, but back from it, to prevent injury in case of handle slippage. If it's difficult to lift the bars, use the tongue jack to raise the tongue slightly.

No fewer than four chain links should be under tension (seven are under tension in Figure 6-4), but you may have to experiment to find which link should be used. It's generally the one that puts the tow vehicle and trailer parallel to the ground when the spring bars are secured. Once the proper link is determined, for future identification, mark the links before and after it with tape or paint (marks on the actual link quickly wear off).

Don't forget to put the handle away after you are finished with it. (When we had a conventional trailer, our practice was to lay the handle across the tongue—just behind the coupler—so that when we made

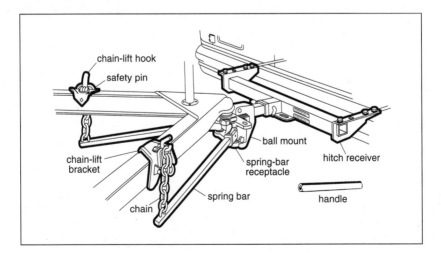

Figure 6-4. *A weight-distributing hitch equalizes the weight between the tow vehicle's front and rear wheels.* (*Courtesy Reese Products*)

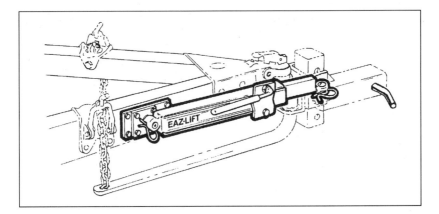

Figure 6-5. *A sway-control bar considerably reduces sway on a conventional trailer.* (Courtesy Eaz-Lift Spring Corporation)

a final check to see that the coupler was latched, we would notice if the handle hadn't been put away.)

Any trailer heavy enough to warrant using a weight-distributing hitch should have a sway-control bar (Figure 6-5); installing it is the next step. One end of the sway-control bar slips over a small ball attached to the side of the tongue, the other end attaches to another ball on the hitch bracket; each is secured with a safety clip. When in place, apply a small amount of tension by turning the handle; don't snug it up too tight. One type of sway-control bar attaches to the spring bars; when the spring bars are in place, the sway-control bar is automatically hooked up. For installation instructions, consult the manual for your particular weight-distributing hitch and sway-control bar.

It's much easier to hitch a fifth-wheel trailer because the hitch is in the bed of a pickup truck (Figure 6-6). The driver of the truck can usually see both the hitch and the pin box, so lining them up is no problem. The actual hitching requires only securing the kingpin in the hitch.

Before backing, open the jaws of the hitch, drop the truck's tailgate (unless it's the notched type that the pin box will clear), and raise the front of the trailer so the bottom of the pin box is just slightly higher than the hitch plate. If the TECC (and breakaway switch lanyard—see page 118) has been coiled around or stowed inside the pin box, uncoil it and let it hang down.

The jaws should automatically come together when the kingpin is solidly in the hitch; if they don't, the safety pin cannot be inserted or, on

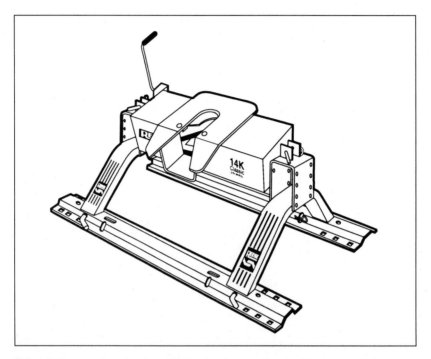

Figure 6-6. *A pedestal-mount fifth-wheel trailer hitch. This type of fifth-wheel hitch is mounted between the wheel wells; another type has supports that fit over the wheel wells.* (Courtesy Reese Products)

some hitches, the locking latch engaged. Usually a slight backward (or forward) movement of the truck closes the jaws; simply putting the tow vehicle in reverse may move it back far enough.

After hitching either type of trailer, attach the breakaway switch lanyard, which sets the trailer's brakes in case of accidental disconnection from the tow vehicle. (Lightweight trailers without electric brakes don't have a breakaway switch.) The switch, located on the trailer tongue or kingpin box, is activated when a pin is pulled from it. The pin is attached to a lanyard, the other end of which has a loop that is put over any handy protrusion on the tow vehicle. (If nothing is handy, install a small hook or an eye bolt.) The lanyard should be loosely secured with some slack, because it takes only a slight strain to pull the pin out—the only time you want this to happen is if the trailer does break away. It's not a good idea to secure the lanyard to the hitch itself; if the hitch becomes disengaged with the breakaway attached to it, no strain would be put on the breakaway switch and it couldn't do its job.

The last step in the hitching process of any trailer is to connect the TECC, making sure the plug is all the way into the socket.

All steps involved in hitching—trailer to tow vehicle, auxiliary vehicle to motorhome—should be included on the checklist described in Chapter 8. Motorhomers should list all additional steps to ready the dinghy for towing, one of which—closing the windows—is often overlooked. Other steps may include disconnecting the driveshaft, installing an axle lock, or putting the dinghy in the proper gear for towing— whatever must be done to prepare your particular brand of auxiliary vehicle for towing (check your owner's manual for this information).

Your RV dealer is a good source of advice about the proper hitch setup for your rig. Another option is to contact a well-established shop that specializes in hitch installations.

If either the tow vehicle or trailer is changed at a later date, the hitch setup may need adjustments or modifications.

Chapter 7

Driving and Handling an RV

A ny experienced driver can drive a motorized RV or a tow vehicle. Driving some self-propelled RVs—camping van conversions, pickup campers, and small Class A and Class C motorhomes—is not much different than driving a car. If a trailer is properly hitched with correct weight distribution, towing should be so effortless that you aren't aware of the trailer. Nevertheless, certain aspects of driving and handling an RV rig are different than driving a car.

Braking and Stopping

It takes considerably longer to bring the extra weight of an RV rig to a stop; the heavier the rig, the longer the distance needed. Get a feel for how long it takes your rig to stop at various speeds before you venture onto a busy highway. On a road with little traffic, but one on which you can travel at highway speeds, practice stopping at different speeds.

As with an automobile, stopping the rig by gradually slowing is better than jamming on the brakes. In certain situations, a quick stop can cause a trailer to jackknife. If the trailer's brakes lock, the breakaway switch may have been activated.

The best way to avoid braking quickly (excluding emergency stops) is to anticipate when braking will be needed and slow down beforehand. On a curve, for instance, especially one with a posted speed limit, slow down well before entering the curve. With an RV rig, it's prudent to cut speed to a little less than the posted limit. Except for telescoping or fold-down units, RVs (especially motorhomes) are top-heavy and can be hard to handle when going too fast around a curve because, once into the curve, the RV is subject to centrifugal force. Heavy braking in this situation also adversely affects handling. If you must brake while in a curve, keep it light. The rear of a trailer tends to swing wider in a curve if bicycles or other heavy objects are stored on the rear bumper.

Brake fade (reduced or nonexistent braking power no matter how much pressure is applied to the brake pedal), which is caused by heat, can occur on a long or steep downgrade if you do not brake judiciously. Apply the brake pedal intermittently—never for longer than a few seconds—because heat builds while the brake pedal is depressed. As the heat buildup intensifies in the pads and linings, the brakes continually lose stopping power until none remains; at this point, no matter how hard the pedal is depressed, nothing will happen. Intermittent application of the brake pedal allows some cooling to take place.

The best technique is to brake as little as possible, yet keep speed low enough so you don't have to ride the brakes hard to slow down. Driver-induced brake fade can also be avoided if you take certain precautions before starting down a grade. At the top of many grades will be a yellow sign (depicting a boxy-looking truck on an incline) warning of a descent, and on steep grades the percentage of the grade and its length may be given (Figure 7-1). For example, a sign may indicate a 6-percent grade for 1 mile. If the grade is steep, long, or both, slow down considerably before beginning the descent; at the same time, shift into second or even first gear. Lower gearing creates drag by working against the compression in the engine, which in turn aids in slowing the vehicle. This effect is more pronounced with a gasoline engine; diesels have much less drag.

Figure 7-1. *A road sign indicating a grade. When the grade is steep, the percentage of the grade is usually provided.*

Starting out slow and braking often for short periods gives the driver some control over the rate at which the speed increases; this is more desirable than starting down at a higher speed and being forced to brake long and hard to slow down.

When towing our trailer, we often pull off the road at the top of a grade, if there is room, and let all traffic go around so we can creep down the hill at the speed we want without holding up anyone. At first, a light tapping of the brakes will slow the rig. As speed slowly increases, unavoidable on many grades, the brakes are applied more frequently with heavier pressure, but only for a few seconds at a time.

If we have been braking considerably on a grade, we'll often resort to using the trailer brake controller to slow the rig. Activating the trailer brakes with the controller's manual override lever a couple of times for 1 or 2 seconds will usually slow the truck. Because the truck's brakes aren't being used, this method allows a little time for them to cool. When trailer brakes are used for slowing, manipulate the manual override lever with a smooth gradual motion to prevent the brakes from locking.

When you test your trailer rig for stopping distances, also try using the controller for slowing and stopping. If the action is too abrupt or not quick enough, the controller must be adjusted. Consult your instruction manual for this simple adjustment.

Motorhomes with a dinghy in tow don't have the benefit of an extra set of brakes because the dinghy's brakes can't be used. The motorhome brakes alone must slow not only the weight of the motorhome but also the thousand pounds or more of the dinghy (unless the dinghy is carried on a tow dolly, which usually has its own brakes). RVers who do a lot of mountain driving might consider installing a brake retarder—a device that provides a steady, controlled downhill speed and slows the vehicle in curves. The regular brakes are bypassed, so no overheating occurs.

Boiling brake fluid, which results when water gets into the fluid, is a less common cause of brake fade. Because brake fluid absorbs water, moisture in the atmosphere can enter the fluid when the reservoir is open. When checking or adding fluid, open the reservoir for the shortest time possible. Once a can of brake fluid is opened, the fluid begins absorbing moisture from the atmosphere. The best practice is to buy the smallest can, use what is needed, discard the remainder, and purchase a new, sealed can to keep on hand for future use.

Trailer Sway

Fifth-wheel trailers and motorhomes normally don't have sway problems, but a conventional trailer can sway when it's moving at highway speeds and being passed by a large truck. Because a truck pushes a large volume of air in front of it, vehicles alongside are affected. The stability of a fifth-wheel trailer lies in the design of the hitch and its location over the truck's rear axle, which limits lateral movement. Because it is a ball, a conventional trailer's hitch contributes to lateral instability, which is further intensified because the hitch is about 5 feet behind the tow vehicle's axle. This arrangement creates two pivot points: the center of the axle and the ball. Even so, any sway will be minimal if a conventional trailer is hitched correctly, a sway-control bar is used, and the weight is distributed properly.

Even if a conventional trailer is relatively unaffected by large trucks passing, the driver of the tow vehicle should never be caught unaware. By constantly monitoring the side mirror, you will know when a truck is about to pass. When this happens, maintain your speed, keep both hands on the wheel, and steer straight. If the trailer begins to sway, never try to correct for the sway by moving the steering wheel; always steer straight ahead. When in this predicament, the natural tendency is to brake and slow down, but this only makes matters worse. In fact, you should increase speed; the acceleration tends to straighten out the trailer. Another straightening procedure is to brake the trailer by using the manual override lever of the brake controller. When the tow vehicle's brake pedal is depressed, the brakes of both the tow vehicle and trailer are activated, but when the manual lever is used, only the trailer brakes are engaged.

Figure 7-2. *A brake controller should be mounted so the driver can reach it easily.*

Applying the manual lever for only an instant usually does the trick. A brake controller should be mounted for easy manual operation—not too far under the dashboard (Figure 7-2).

An auxiliary vehicle towed by a motorhome isn't affected by passing trucks because it doesn't have the long, high, solid area as does the side of a conventional trailer.

Wind

Strong crosswinds can also cause sway, but the problem won't be severe if the trailer is hitched properly and weight is distributed correctly.

Although a motorhome or fifth-wheel trailer can't sway in the manner of a conventional trailer, high crosswinds exert considerable force on the rig and affect the steering. Keep both hands on the wheel and reduce speed when it's windy.

Be alert for signs warning of windy conditions ahead. Be prepared for the full force of the wind after exiting a tunnel, at the end of a road cut between high banks, and after passing around a hill or a sheltering line of trees.

Length and Weight Considerations

Except for camping van conversions and pickup campers, any RV rig is longer than the vehicles you may be used to driving. Always keep this extra length in mind because it affects turning corners, changing lanes, and making U-turns.

Length is not a problem on highway curves because they are designed so trucks can traverse them, but it can be a problem when making 90-degree right turns on city streets. To make the turn without running up over the curb, swing the rig wide by pulling straight ahead into the intersection before making the turn. With a very long rig, it may be necessary to pull into the lane to the left of the desired lane and then swing back into it (Figure 7-3). If there are vehicles in the lane to the left, of course, this maneuver can't be made. In that case, the driver can go over the curb or wait until there is no other traffic to contend with, which will certainly irritate any drivers behind you. Because swinging wide is necessary, watch for drivers who are also turning and who intend to cut inside your rig on the right.

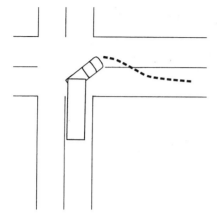

Figure 7-3. *Making a right turn with a long RV sometimes requires swinging wide, perhaps into the oncoming traffic lane. The dashed line indicates the turning path of the tow vehicle/ trailer.*

Making a 90-degree left turn is not so restrictive because the rig necessarily swings fairly wide; however, be careful to swing wide enough to avoid vehicles stopped in the street you are entering. With motorhomes that have long rear overhangs, the driver must be careful when turning to ensure that sign posts, mailboxes, and guy wires are clear of the rear as it swings wide.

Fifth-wheel trailers make the sharpest U-turns. Our 29-foot fifth-wheel, starting out from the shoulder on a highway, requires only two lanes for a U-turn, yet we could never make a U-turn in this space with our 23-foot conventional trailer. Large motorhomes towing an auxiliary vehicle may need as many as seven lanes. It is important to know how much space your rig needs to execute a U-turn.

A word of caution: Fifth-wheels can make such tight turns because the trailer pivots on its tires. A tight turn made too quickly can roll the tires off the rims, so make these turns at the slowest speed possible. Watching the tires in the mirror may give you pause because they become distorted during the turn.

Make allowances for the length of the rig whenever changing lanes. When passing another vehicle on two-lane highways, there must be sufficient room for your rig to enter the passing lane. Oncoming traffic must be at least a half-mile away to allow enough time to move well ahead of the vehicle you are passing to give you enough space to bring your rig safely back into the right lane. Be sure you put your rig well behind any vehicle in front of you, and always maintain this space to allow enough room for an emergency stop.

Some motorhomers, like truckers, sit so high above the pavement that small cars in the blind spot on the right go unnoticed. Wait until the vehicle being passed is visible in the right mirror and you are well ahead of it before cutting back into the right lane.

Unless you intend to keep moving faster than the other traffic, passing is not usually necessary. Other drivers don't like following an RV and will try to pass you. Don't fight it; just let them pass and be on their way. Be on the lookout for impatient drivers who pass in a no-passing zone. When this happens to us, we always slow down considerably—if we can—so the passer can get around us faster. Because of the restricted sight line, the passer could collide with oncoming traffic, so slowing down may keep our rig from being involved. Never increase your speed while another vehicle is passing, except to control sway.

When piloting an RV rig, it's especially important never to change lanes or turn unless the turn signals are on well in advance of the move. Keep in mind that signaling doesn't give you the right to make any maneuver; it's merely to let other drivers know your intentions. Don't assume, however, that other drivers will respect your intentions. Be on the alert for drivers who suddenly pull out to pass just after you signal to move into the passing lane. Always shut off the turn signals immediately after completing any maneuver.

You will have to adjust to the acceleration of your rig, which, because of its weight, is considerably slower than that of a car or truck. This has a bearing on passing when fast acceleration is required, as well as when entering a high-speed highway from a ramp. The safest way to merge into the flow of traffic is to enter the highway at the same speed the traffic is moving, but most RV rigs can't get up to this speed in the length of a typical entrance ramp. Shifting to second gear may provide extra power. If a good ramp speed is achieved, it may be necessary to slow down when heavy traffic doesn't allow enough space for the rig to merge. Acceleration from a dead stop can be very slow with heavy rigs. Carefully evaluate every entry onto high-speed highways.

Overhead Clearances

RVers with telescoping and folding tent trailers are the only RVers who don't have to be concerned about overhead clearances because their units are about the same height or lower than the tow vehicle. All other RVers should measure their units so the exact height is known. (Tip: Write the height on a label and stick it on the dashboard.) Interstate and other major highways have enough overpass clearance for the tallest trucks, so RVs also have enough clearance. It is on secondary highways where clearances can be too low. Once we were following the directory instructions to a city campground and, after turning a corner, were confronted with an underpass a block ahead with a 10-foot clearance—too low for our trailer's 11-foot, 2-inch height. After a moment of shock, we realized that the entrance to the campground was just before the underpass. Another time, we met an RVer who drove through an underpass that was too low for his trailer; the roof air conditioner and a lightweight motorcycle stored on the roof were swept off, taking the roof rack and ladder along with them.

Tunnels and certain bridges with curved structural supports over the roadway often have a lower clearance on the outside edge than at the center (Figure 7-4).

The height of a rig may preclude its being taken on some ferries. Before we were allowed on a ferry with a 12-foot-height limit, an attendant measured our trailer with an inverted L-shaped length of plastic pipe. He assured us that if the trailer fit under the pipe, which it did with a few inches to spare, it would fit on the ferry. It seemed like awfully close quarters, but the trailer did fit.

If you refuel at truckstops with covered islands, the overhead clearance is sufficient for any RV rig, but be careful at service stations with covered islands if the overhead clearance isn't posted. Buildings with projecting eaves and signs can also be hazards.

Keep an eye out for low tree branches in campgrounds. We have encountered them numerous times. In one instance, we rounded a curve and found we couldn't continue to the sites farther ahead because of low-hanging branches. We had to back out a considerable and curvy distance, and settle for a less desirable site. Another time, in a public campground, we encountered branches too low to clear. We moved the trailer close enough so that one of us could climb onto the trailer's roof and saw off the branches.

Mirrors

Truckers check their mirrors about every 30 seconds, a good habit RVers should develop: An overtaking vehicle won't ever be a surprise, and you can put both hands on the wheel well before the bow-wave air pressure of a passing truck affects your rig.

Although the primary function of mirrors is to keep track of traffic

Figure 7-4. *When driving an RV rig, be aware of overhead clearances. Some bridges and tunnels have two clearances posted.*

behind and alongside, they should also be used to check on the RV. When we use the mirrors to make frequent checks on our trailer, we look at the trailer tires to see that they are maintaining the proper inflation and there are no other obvious tire problems. We also watch for smoke emanating from the wheel areas, which may indicate a brake problem or, worse, a fire in a wheel bearing. The attitude of the trailer is also checked. One time we noticed that the trailer was leaning to one side. We stopped immediately and found a broken spring before it had caused any significant damage. Frequent mirror checks often reveal problems before they become serious.

The trailer tires aren't visible when the trailer is directly in line behind the tow vehicle, but going around a curve brings them into view. If we want to check the tires on a straight road, we make a shallow "S" maneuver while staying in our lane; the tires can be seen as the trailer swings slightly out of line.

If you suspect a problem, don't rely solely on the mirrors; stop the rig as soon as safely possible and get out and make an inspection. If someone behind repeatedly honks, or honks when passing, don't assume it's just another irritated driver. The other driver may be trying to call your attention to a problem with your rig.

Urban Driving

Driving a rig on an urban interstate highway system can be a harrowing experience, but less so if you prepare for the trip beforehand and follow certain practices.

First, plan ahead. Before using a city interstate highway, get as detailed a map of the city as you can find. For our urban transits, we generally use a city map, an area map, and a Triptik map (available to AAA members). We especially like Triptiks because they indicate exit numbers and have enough detail so we can determine whether an exit is a standard right exit or one requiring the use of the left lane. (Other maps may or may not include exit numbers.)

Preplanning includes locating your exits on the map. Note the exit number and the name of the street or the highway number at the exit. On an interstate, watch for the first sign for your exit; advance knowledge allows enough time to shift lanes safely, if necessary, well ahead of the exit.

If you miss your exit, go to the next one; don't try to recover by stopping, slowing down, or backing up. Most urban exits are designed so that you can exit the highway, cross over or under it, reenter it going in the opposite direction, and return to the missed exit. Most city exits aren't far apart, so little time will be lost. Exiting the interstate is the only safe maneuver, even if you have to drive some distance before you can reverse your direction.

If you are moving slowly, stay in the right lane; however, driving an RV rig is usually easier in the lane second from the right. In this lane, traffic entering the interstate is avoided and, because most exit-only lanes are in the right lane, you won't be forced into an unplanned exit. In the second lane from the right, your rig won't block the view of entering drivers. If you drive in the far-left lane, your speed has to match that of other vehicles in this high-speed lane, so avoid it as much as possible.

Following too closely is the main cause of accidents on most city interstate highways. It is especially important that RVers allow plenty of stopping space between their rig and the vehicle in front.

Don't travel over or under the posted maximum and minimum speed limits on a city interstate. If other drivers are exceeding the speed limit, give them every opportunity to pass you on the left, but don't join in the race. Anyone who wants to drive below the minimum posted limit shouldn't drive on such a highway.

Be sure you have sufficient fuel before entering a city interstate. Shoulders don't usually exist on these busy thoroughfares, and stopping for any reason can be hazardous to you and your rig, as well as other vehicles.

Urban highway driving is easier at certain times of the day. We never tow our trailer anywhere near a city interstate highway during the morning or evening rush hours. When we must drive on a city highway, we always arrange to leave late and arrive early, timing our passage to occur during lunch time, from about 11:30 A.M. to 1:00 P.M. Less traffic in general, and less truck traffic in particular, is on the highway during these hours.

When we stay at a campground outside a city and have no choice but to leave using a route that takes us through or around the city on a high-speed highway, we generally scout out the route before we have our trailer in tow, noting the number of lanes and where they increase or decrease, left exits, and busy interchanges.

Sometimes we must use urban highways, but whenever possible

we go out of our way to avoid them by taking secondary roads well outside city limits. These circuitous routes may put us a good many miles outside a city, but we think the extra time is a worthwhile tradeoff for safer and less stressful driving.

Parking

Parking an RV rig in a large lot such as those found at shopping centers and supermarkets is usually no problem. If, however, the lot has islands or dividers separating each row, the parking spaces are usually unsuitable for towed RVs and most motorhomes, and the sharp turn required at the end to enter a row is often too tight for most RV rigs to negotiate.

An open lot with parking spaces delineated by painted lines is the best for RVs. Many RV rigs take up two spaces, and some extend beyond the boundaries of the two. If possible, RVers with long rigs should park far away from other cars so drivers aren't forced to go around either the front or rear of an overhanging rig; in doing so, the driver's view is partially blocked and other vehicles on the roadway may not be visible.

Always consider how you will get out of a spot before parking the rig: Will other vehicles that come in after you block your exit? We always try to park at the outer end of a row, near an exit, with the rig facing in the direction of the exit. If the road around the lot is wide enough and there isn't much traffic, we often park on the right side of the perimeter road instead. When we park in a restaurant lot, we try to arrive before or after rush hours to avoid the crowd. If we arrive before the rush hours, however, we are careful to park where we won't be boxed in by others who arrive later.

If any parking lot is unsuitable for your rig, perhaps a parking place on the street can be found. Our rig fits into two parallel parking spaces and we often find street parking that is easy to maneuver into. Again, park the rig where your exit can't be blocked.

When parking a conventional trailer next to a curb, keep the tires well away from the curb. Otherwise, when leaving the parking space, if you can't pull straight ahead and angle out into the street gradually, the trailer wheels will turn into the curb.

It's the rare big city that has any parking spaces for an RV rig, so it's best not to take it into a city. Instead, leave the RV in a nearby campground and travel into the city in your tow vehicle or dinghy—or take advantage of mass transportation and bus tours.

Backing a Trailer

We will attempt to do the difficult, perhaps the impossible, by using words to describe how to back a trailer. The words, however, only give you information about basic backing procedures; the way to become an expert is by practicing.

A common instruction for backing a trailer is: Place one hand at the bottom of the steering wheel, then turn the wheel in the direction you want the back end of the trailer to go. We think this emphasizes hand placement when trailer movement is more important. You can maneuver the trailer no matter where your hands are on the wheel, so put your hands where they are comfortable, then use the side mirror to focus your attention on the rear of the trailer.

There are two important steps in backing: (1) The trailer must be started turning in the proper direction; and (2) once the rig is turning, it must be straightened out because, when straight, the driver has maximum control for turning the rig.

Let's assume there are no ditches, tree branches, or other hazards and you can back straight into the site. Put the tow vehicle in reverse and begin backing s-l-o-w-l-y, very slowly, never taking your eyes from the view of the rear of the trailer in the mirror.

When backing straight, the trailer quickly begins to turn one way or the other, even if the tow vehicle and trailer were lined up straight at the beginning. Watch the rear of the trailer; if it begins to move to the right, turn the steering wheel slowly, smoothly, and slightly to the right—just enough to realign the trailer with the tow vehicle. Repeat the maneuver when the rear of the trailer begins to turn to the left by steering to the left. Continue turning left to right, right to left, until the trailer is in the site. The steering wheel should be in nearly constant but slow motion as you turn it slightly and then bring it back.

When backing, many trailerists tend to make steering corrections too quickly. It takes a few feet of travel for the trailer to react to the movement of the steering wheel, so do not turn the wheel too much for correcting.

When the trailer cannot be backed straight into a site, the procedure is different: To start the trailer turning left, you must steer right, and vice versa. When the trailer begins to turn, holding the steering wheel steady does not cause the trailer to continue in a nice easy arc into the site. If the wheel is held in position, the turn becomes tighter and tighter until the trailer jackknifes. Constant steering-wheel correction in both directions is necessary when backing and turning, just as when backing straight. Turning the steering wheel in the same direction the rear of the trailer is going straightens out the rig.

An important aspect of successful backing is pulling forward. This is a vital maneuver when backing into any site that requires turning the trailer. When the rear of the trailer begins to veer toward one side as you are backing and turning, straighten the rig by pulling forward a few feet. Each forward movement makes the next backing movement straighter. This takes a lot of patience at some sites: We were once assigned a site situated at a 90-degree angle to a narrow access road. Trees lined both sides of the site, which was also narrow, and there was a steep, 5-foot-high terrace on the far side of the road opposite the site's entrance. Had the site been properly angled, we could have backed into it without any problem, but, with the trees—which necessitated turning sharply to avoid them—and the terrace—which severely restricted forward movement—maneuvering into it took more than a half hour. Since there was only about 3 feet for pulling forward, we went back and forth about 20 times.

Fifth-wheels turn much more quickly than conventional trailers when backing, thus requiring more pulling-forward movements. Incidentally, if a fifth-wheel is difficult to back, the hitch may not be properly positioned relative to the tow vehicle's rear axle. The center of the jaws should be about 2 inches forward of the center of the axle; this puts some of the hitch weight on the front wheels of the tow vehicle. If the hitch is behind the axle, the front-wheel load is lightened and steering is affected.

Backing a trailer is like any other acquired skill: The more you practice, the easier it is and the better you become.

Driving in Inclement Weather

When driving an RV rig in rain, snow, and fog, take the same precautions as when driving in ideal conditions, only more so:

• Reduce speed.

• Maintain more space between your rig and the vehicle in front of you.

• Allow more distance for stopping.

If speed is reduced on wet roads, the rig behaves better and the driver has more time to react.

Visibility is reduced in bad weather and certain conditions can play tricks with vision. This can affect both you and the driver in front of you, so stay well behind the vehicle ahead to allow for its sudden movements, slowing, or stopping.

Rain, ice, and snow make roads slick, so stopping requires more distance. Brake gently on a slick surface; slamming on the brakes results in sliding. RVs with the best traction are those with heavy weight on the rear wheels: motorhomes, especially those with dual rear wheels; pickup campers; and camping van conversions. When these RVs begin to skid, however, they are very difficult to control.

When traveling, pay attention to weather forecasts. If severe weather is predicted, it may be wise to stay where you are and wait it out. There is a bonus about RVing and bad weather: If you are on the road when conditions warrant halting traffic, you can be warm, safe, and comfortable in your RV and rely on your food and water supply until you can move on.

Stretching Fuel Dollars

One method of reducing fuel consumption is to reduce the RV's weight by not hauling unneeded items. Also, make sure the maintenance on your vehicle is always up to date. Keep the engine tuned, replace fuel and air filters when dirty, and inflate tires to the proper pressure. Fuel dollars go even farther if certain driving practices are followed.

It's almost impossible to make jackrabbit starts with any type of RV rig, so don't waste fuel trying. Use a steady, firm depression of the throttle when accelerating after a stop.

The faster the rig is driven, the more fuel it consumes. Driving at 65 mph uses 35 percent more fuel than driving at 55 mph. For example, if a motorhome averages 10 miles to the gallon at 55 mph, the cost of fuel is $1.25 a gallon, and 500 miles are driven, fuel costs would be $62.50; at 65 mph, fuel costs would increase to $84.38—a difference

Table 7-1. Comparison of Fuel Costs at Different Speeds

Distance	Speed (mph)	Fuel Rate (mpg)	Gallons Consumed	Cost per Gallon	Total Cost of Fuel
500 miles	55	10.0	50.0	$1.25	$62.50
500 miles	65	7.4	67.5	$1.25	$84.38

Note:
   These are hypothetical examples. Actual fuel consumption figures will vary considerably depending on engine size, whether the engine is gas or diesel, transmission type, rear-axle ratio, highway speed, gross combined vehicle weight rating, actual weight of the RV, tire size and inflation pressure, temperature, individual driving habits, and type of terrain.

of $21.88 (Table 7-1). Project this over the miles driven in a year and you could save hundreds of dollars by simply driving a little slower. Initially, if you plan short days' runs, you shouldn't be tempted to drive faster to shave a few minutes off your arrival time.

When driving at highway speeds, let the cruise control take care of the throttle; it hasn't the human tendency to continually speed up and slow down. A cruise control maintains even, steady speeds, with resultant fuel economy. When approaching a hill, a situation that the cruise control can't anticipate, the driver should take over and accelerate somewhat before the hill is reached.

When climbing grades, fuel is saved when second gear or even first, rather than third, is used. For many RV rigs, trying to accelerate on grades is wasted effort, hence wasted fuel. Manually downshift, let the speed drop, and save on fuel, as well as engine and transmission wear and tear.

Although driving in overdrive saves fuel, most manufacturers do not recommend using this gear when towing. Check the owner's manual for information on how to use this gear.

Driving into head winds increases fuel consumption, but tail winds provide a boost. On Interstate 80 across Wyoming, the prevailing wind is westerly and usually strong. When we travel this route into the wind, we have noticed that the fuel gauge drops rapidly, but heading east, fuel consumption improves markedly.

Air flow affects fuel consumption. For the best fuel economy, air should have an unimpeded flow over and around the rig. Side mirrors are a necessary impediment, but they contribute to increased fuel consumption, as do running boards, storage pods, roof-mounted horns, and cargo carried on the roof.

A conventional or fifth-wheel trailer improperly hitched or loaded with the front higher than the rear or vice versa is as far from being aerodynamic as possible. The air rushing by swirls around underneath in the jumble of piping, jacks, holding tanks, and chassis frame members, creating enough resistance to act like a brake. An enclosed underbody (a feature of many late-model trailers), with the trailer properly hitched or loaded so it is parallel to the ground, offers the least wind resistance.

Driving Etiquette

Most RVers are courteous, but you will occasionally encounter some who have bad driving manners. Inconsiderate RVers drive as if they are the only ones on the road, never giving a thought to how their actions affect other drivers. Special problems do exist with RVs in certain highway situations, but they should not be made worse by bad driving manners.

When driving our rig, we have as much right as anyone to be on the highway; nevertheless, our basic driving philosophy is to defer to other drivers. Speeding down the highway is no time to vie with others for the meaningless honor of being king of the road or leader of the pack. We are perfectly satisfied to let everyone else pass us if they are traveling at a higher speed.

On interstate highways with a top speed limit of 65 mph and 55 mph for trucks, we usually travel about 50 mph. At that speed, driving is less stressful because big trucks can pass us without having to speed up and cars can whiz around us. If the interstate is crowded, as it often is through cities, and lane-switching is a problem, we kick up the speed to the top limit for trucks while in the congested area.

On two-lane roads, we sometimes don't have the option of driving at a lower speed if we want to be considerate of other drivers. If the road has few passing opportunities, we maintain the speed limit until we reach a place where other vehicles can pass. Then, if traffic allows, we slow down considerably so vehicles can get around us quickly. If several vehicles are behind us in a no-passing zone, we try to get off the road to let them by. If the shoulder is wide enough and suitable, we signal, slow down, and pull off, or if we see a spacious area or a U-shaped driveway at a business or a large parking lot, we may get off the road completely. Of course, in states that provide them, we use the slow-vehicle lane and turnouts.

Drivers are often impatient when they are behind an RV rig, especially on a hill on a two-lane highway with no passing lane, because almost every RV rig loses speed when going up hills. Unless the rig can be moved onto the shoulder, nothing can be done about this situation, so watch carefully for drivers who may make unsafe moves to get around you.

Enter an interstate highway as close to the speed limit as possible. This causes fewer problems for drivers entering behind you. Be alert for drivers who speed by on either side of the entrance to reach the highway before your rig—a dangerous maneuver that can adversely affect several vehicles.

Use directional signals when turning or changing lanes, pulling off onto the shoulder, and moving back onto the highway.

Many RVers look upon truck drivers as adversaries, but most are courteous and considerate as long as RVers treat them the same way. We consider truck drivers to be people at work with a schedule to meet, so we try not to interfere with them as they do their job. We make it easy for trucks to pass us by slowing down and moving to the right; we much prefer being passed than having a monster truck tailgating, waiting for an opportunity to get around us.

Overheating

Motorhomes and vehicles with a factory tow package are equipped with a transmission oil cooler and, in most normal driving conditions—even on upgrades—overheating shouldn't occur unless the RV is overloaded or insects are clogging the radiator.

If overheating occurs, most likely it will be in hot weather when climbing a grade. Turning off the air conditioner may reduce the overheating; shifting to a lower gear also helps. If these procedures do not work, pull off the road, put the gearshift lever in park, set the parking brake, leave the engine on, and raise the hood. Next, apply a little throttle to get as much air as possible through the radiator. Watch the temperature gauge as you are applying the throttle. When it drops back to a normal level and stays there when the throttle is released, it should be safe to proceed. With this method it takes about 15 minutes for the engine to cool. Don't touch the radiator or any engine parts; they are hot enough to cause a bad burn.

Flat Tires

If a flat tire occurs on any type of motorhome or tow vehicle during driving, it will be felt immediately in the steering wheel, but a flat on a trailer can go unnoticed unless it is seen in the mirror. When you sense that a tire has gone flat, keep a good grip on the wheel, slow down gradually, and try to park on the shoulder. If the rig can't be parked completely off the road, put out warning devices. Reflective triangles are best; in some states it's illegal to use flares. Put the transmission in park and set the parking brake firmly before chocking the wheels. Never fail to chock both the front and rear wheels before attempting to change a tire. Place the jack so that when raised, it rests against the frame of the RV or tow vehicle; don't put it under a bumper. Check the owner's manual for specific jacking instructions. If the person changing the tire is exposed to traffic, another person should be stationed well behind the rig to wave the traffic around.

Those with a large motorhome may not be able to change a tire and often require assistance. A road service organization has the heavy-duty equipment needed for jacking up such units and handling the big tires. RVers with smaller units can carry the equipment needed to change flats themselves.

A good jack should be the primary piece of tire-changing equipment. A hydraulic jack is the easiest to use; it requires much less effort than the worm-gear jack typically supplied with vehicles. A hydraulic jack should be checked periodically and replaced if it is leaking. Be sure your jack has a lifting capacity higher than the weight of your RV or tow vehicle.

If the flat has caused the vehicle to be so low that the jack won't fit under it, place a leveling board (see Chapter 8) in front of the wheel with the flat, and drive slowly onto the board. This should raise the axle high enough to slip a jack under it. When a flat occurs on dual wheels, the unaffected tire can be positioned on the leveling board and a jack may not be needed. This technique can also be used on trailers with two axles. If the flat is on the rear wheel of a truck towing a fifth-wheel trailer, unhitch the trailer so the jack won't also have to lift the weight of the trailer.

Instead of a lug wrench, which doesn't provide much leverage, RVers with pickup trucks and mid-size or larger motorhomes and trailers should consider carrying a ¾-inch breaker bar with a socket that fits the lug nuts or lug bolts (trailer wheels have lug bolts) on their vehicle. Loosening the nuts or bolts is much easier with a breaker bar; with the great leverage, they can also be tightened more securely.

Check all spares frequently to ensure they are properly inflated.

Navigation

In our rig, the copilot can't just sit back and relax. He or she is responsible for navigating so the driver can concentrate on the traffic. The navigator is most useful when driving on a congested highway through an unfamiliar city.

Well before we reach a city, we have all the necessary maps ready for instant consultation. Hurtling along a traffic-clogged, multi-lane highway is not the time to be unfolding and refolding maps.

Once in the city or its outskirts, the navigator's responsibilities include checking the lane to the right when the driver needs to make a lane change in that direction and, when the rig is in the far right lane, apprising the driver of entering vehicles. The navigator carefully watches highway signs to remind the driver about upcoming exit-only lanes (so the driver can move out of the lane if not exiting), a left exit lane (if that is the desired exit), junctions with other highways (where there may be increased exiting and entering traffic), and, if leaving the highway, the distance to the desired exit. The driver makes judgments based on what the navigator says.

The navigator also guides the driver to the campground. Prior to entering an unfamiliar metropolitan area, we use campground directories to find a place to stay. If there are several campgrounds that appeal to us, we circle the exact locations on the street map of the city. In the directory, an ad for a campground may include a map, which can be helpful; the page on which the selected campgrounds are listed is marked with a bookmark for quick consultation later.

Directions to a campground may read something like this: "From

Exit 10, E on frontage road 1 mi.; S on Highway 463 2.8 mi., W on Elm St. 1.5 mi." Well ahead of Exit 10, the navigator opens the directory to the page with the campground listing. In plenty of time to make necessary lane changes, the navigator reminds the driver about the approaching exit. Immediately after exiting, the driver tells the navigator the last three digits on the odometer—let's say 48.7. Consulting the directions to the campground, the navigator says: "Go straight ahead on the frontage road and turn right on Highway 463. The odometer should then read 49.7." When the turn is made, the driver's next instruction is "At odometer reading 52.5, turn right on Elm Street." Next, the driver receives the final odometer reading, 54.0, which should be at the campground.

When a detailed street map is used, the navigator tells the driver in advance the name of the street where a turn must be made, how many blocks away it is, which way to turn, and—something we find helpful—the name of the street immediately preceding the desired street.

For navigating, we keep handy in the cockpit a magnifying glass for reading small print on maps, a pen or pencil for mileage calculations, and a penlight. A dashboard-mounted compass is useful, if it can be corrected for magnetic influences; other types are not accurate.

Some children can navigate to the campground, but if they're not old enough to drive, they don't have the experience to navigate on the highway.

In addition to other duties, the navigator is responsible for using the side mirror to make frequent checks on the curb side of the rig.

Additional Driving Tips and Information

When driving an RV rig, you will have to make frequent refueling stops, so allow extra time for travel. Taking additional breaks every few hours provides a beneficial rest for the rig and its occupants. Tires have a chance to cool, and people and pets can get some exercise. Whenever you stop, look under a motorized vehicle for leaks, inspect a trailer's suspension system, and check the condition of all tires—touch them to see if they are hotter than they should be. If so, a serious problem may exist that will have to be fixed before the rig can be safely driven farther. If a burning smell is detected, trace down its source as quickly as possible, and have a fire extinguisher ready in case actual flames appear.

When stopped on an upgrade, be prepared for the rig to drift backward slightly before it moves forward.

Don't take your rig where a sign indicates that the road ahead is unsuitable for RVs or there is no RV turnaround.

Be wary of taking your rig on unfamiliar backwoods roads; you may get into a serious predicament—bogged down in mud or dust, trapped by obstacles, unable to proceed because of rocks or ruts in the road, or bridges that can't bear the weight of your rig. Seasoned RVers scout out an unfamiliar backwoods road before taking their rig on it.

On a multi-lane highway, don't travel at the same speed as the vehicles on your left, in front, and behind; you are boxed in and have nowhere to go in an emergency. Slow down, if you can safely do so, just enough to allow the vehicle on the left to get ahead of you; this also may encourage the driver of the vehicle behind to pass.

Try to avoid short, steep inclines, such as at the entrances to some parking lots and service stations. With fifth-wheel trailers, the underside of the gooseneck may rub the top of the sides of the truckbed just after reaching the top of the incline; if any RV is low to the ground, its rear may scrape.

Chapter 8

Selecting a Campground Site and Using the Hookups

All campgrounds should be built so sites are accessible and the hookups well-placed and obvious. A good many of them are, so setting up is straightforward, and even a beginner should have no problems. In your travels, however, you are bound to find campsites that fall far short of being perfect. The types of sites and hookup arrangements you will most likely encounter are described in this chapter.

Site Selection

Site selection is not as important for an overnight stay as it is for a longer period, but you will always want a site long enough for your RV, and one into which it can be easily maneuvered. If a campground is not too crowded, you may be able to select your own site; otherwise, a site will be assigned. At the entrance to some campgrounds, you can see how the sites are arranged; in others, none of the sites, or only a few, are visible. If you are assigned a site that you can't see from where you are registering, take a look at it before putting your rig into it. If the assigned site is not to your liking and others are vacant, request a different site.

When site selection is up to you, first drive through the campground and look over the sites, if possible. Most private campgrounds have interior roads that can be negotiated by RVs of all sizes and types, but this is not always the case in public campgrounds: roads may not be wide enough, curves may be so tight that long RVs can't make the turn, and low branches that could scrape the roof may overhang the road. These circumstances occur most often in national forest campgrounds, many of which were built long ago when tent camping was more common than RVing. Before taking our rig into a campground where we are doubtful about accessibility, we park at the entrance and walk through the campground looking for trouble spots.

Sites in any campground are either the back-in or pull-through type. Pull-throughs may be straight or curved. Unless a back-in site is angled properly to the road, it may be impossible to maneuver a mid-size or large rig into it. For maneuvering into a back-in site at a 90-degree angle to the road, the road should be wide enough so the front of the rig can swing onto the far side of the road as the turn into the site is made. Backing a trailer into a site is easier if there is road space in front of the site; this enables you to pull the trailer ahead a few times to straighten it out during the backing process.

Some sites are angled at more than 90 degrees from the direction of travel. The greater the angle, whether the site is to the right or left of the road, the easier it is to back into. If the angle is less than 90 degrees from the direction of travel, however, it is virtually impossible to back a trailer or any but the tiniest motorhome into it (Figure 8-1). Sometimes a self-propelled RV can be headed into rather than backed into such a site, but hookups will probably be on the wrong side. It is easier to back into a site on the left side of the road than on the right because the driver has better visibility of the site during backing.

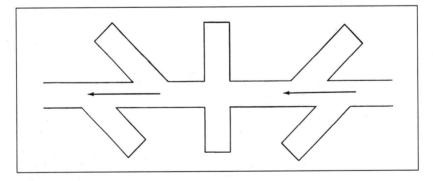

Figure 8-1. *Traveling in the direction of the arrows, it is easiest to back into the angled sites on the lower left and upper right, but maneuvering any RV rig into the angled sites opposite these two is very difficult. The difficulty of getting into the sites 90 degrees to the road depends on how wide the road is; a wider road makes it easier.*

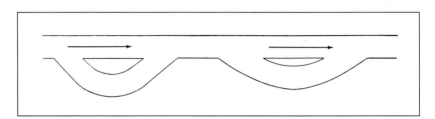

Figure 8-2. *The curved pull-through site on the left is too tight for large RVs. The shallower curve on the right is better.*

To maneuver large Class A motorhomes and trailers into a curved pull-through, the curve should be shallow; however, many pull-throughs are too sharply curved for large RVs (Figure 8-2). When we must park in such a site, after first determining whether the site is large enough and obstruction-free, the trailer is backed in from the upper end of the site rather than pulled forward from the lower end. This way, the rig doesn't have to negotiate the sharply curved portion. After unhitching, the truck is parked behind the trailer.

In some campgrounds, the delineation of sites presents a problem for RVers. Ideally, anything marking the site—posts, poles, logs, railroad ties, boulders, concrete curbs, fencing, trees, shrubbery—should be at least 4 feet from the site proper so nothing interferes with backing or pulling in. Even a post bearing the campsite number should not be right on the front corner of the site. Be alert for anything you could bump into when maneuvering into a site. Some campgrounds have sites in various lengths and configurations. Trailerists should select a site long enough for both the trailer and the tow vehicle.

As for hookups, some campgrounds may have a variety of arrangements: some sites with full hookups, some with just electricity and water, and some with no hookups. The hookups determine the rates. If you stay in such a campground only overnight, and you want hookups but don't need to empty the holding tanks, it is more economical to take a site with just electricity and water. In some public campgrounds where there are no hookups, the sites are undelineated; RVs can be parked any place, facing in any direction.

Keep these points in mind when choosing a site:

• The site must be sufficiently wide and long to accommodate your rig. If your RV has an awning or slideout, be sure it can be extended without encroaching on adjacent sites or hitting obstacles such as trees, shrubbery, and wires.

• The site should be reasonably level, not only from side-to-side but also from front to back.

• Hookups should be conveniently located.

• Pay attention to how the site is oriented to the sun. If you don't want the sun to shine in the door, park where the door faces north, but keep in mind that the sun may then fall on the side where the refrigerator is located. If the refrigerator side is unshaded and the outside temperature is hot, the refrigerator may not cool efficiently.

• If you want to use the campground showers, you may want a site near the washroom. We always use our own facilities, so we prefer a location where other campers don't have to trek through or around our site on their way to the washroom.

• In a tree-shaded site, check for branches that are too low for the height of your rig or that would interfere with the TV antenna when it is raised. Consider if branches may blow down in a windstorm; dead branches, particularly, may cause problems. In a gentle breeze, branches—even leaves—touching the side of the RV can make fine scratches in the finish.

• Consider the site's relationship to a river or stream. We once had to leave a campground because of its riverside location. We knew when we parked in a site next to the river that a heavy rain could cause flooding. It did rain, and it did flood, but the flooding was gradual enough that we had time to get out before the water rose high enough to imperil our rig. Since then, when we camp near a river or stream, we always ask the campground manager about possible flooding. We can handle gradual flooding because we have time to move our RV, but we don't stay in places subject to flash flooding, particularly dry washes in desert areas.

• A well-lit campground is desirable, but be aware of the placement of the lights. A light directly over a transparent bedroom roof vent or outside a bedroom window may interfere with your sleep.

• End sites are often the most desirable in a campground, especially those where the RV's door opens on the side facing away from other sites. This provides more privacy and sometimes a nice view.

- Consider structures near the site. A nearby building may block breezes. If the structure is light-colored, it can reflect an unpleasant brightness, as well as heat, into the RV.

- After trying to find everything else you want in a campsite, don't forget to consider the view from the windows.

Leveling

If you have a trailer, make sure the unit is level after you've maneuvered into the campsite but before unhitching it. If the site is well designed, you won't have to level the RV; if it's not, leveling devices will be needed under the RV's wheels. Refrigerators in older RVs do not work properly unless the freezer compartment is level; with newer refrigerators, leveling isn't as critical. Even so, the RV should be level for your comfort (so the bed doesn't slope, for example).

Class A motorhomes and some trailers can be equipped with automatic levelers. With these, leveling of a motorhome is done from the cockpit; a trailer's leveler control is inside the trailer. Unless your RV is so equipped, you will have to do the leveling as most RVers do—by manually inserting leveling devices under the wheels to elevate the unit. Having the right leveling equipment—a bubble level and either boards or special leveling devices, which can be purchased at RV supply stores—and keeping it in a convenient place make leveling a quick and easy job.

Although we have a newer refrigerator that doesn't need critical leveling, we initially used the leveled refrigerator as a basis for finding a location to place the bubble level elsewhere in the RV when setting up (a hangover from the old days, we presume). This is the procedure: Place a bubble level in the refrigerator at a 90-degree angle to the sides of the RV. To center the bubble, level the unit by placing boards under the wheels on the low side to raise the RV the appropriate amount. Motorhomes and other self-propelled RVs may need levelers under both the front and back wheels on the low side. Next, remove the level and find a place on or in the RV where the bubble is centered as it was in the refrigerator—ideally, where the level can be conveniently used when setting up. On one of our trailers, this location was just inside the door, on the floor. The vinyl floor covering provided a smooth base for the level. On our fifth-wheel, this area is unusable because it's carpeted, so the level is placed on a 9-inch piece of 1 x 2 wood attached to the back of the dinette seat, which is just inside the door. The board is positioned to correspond to the refrigerator when it is level.

A place to set the level for fore-and-aft leveling must also be found. On our trailer, the metal doorsill is parallel to the fore-and-aft leveling surface of the refrigerator. This is convenient because both leveling positions can be checked while standing outside the open door.

So far, we've been discussing portable rather than permanently mounted levels, but small levels that attach to the outside of RVs with double-faced tape are available. If used, two levels are needed, one for each leveling plane. They are difficult to align when installing, and hot weather may cause them to shift position, so they can't be relied on for accuracy. Alignment is even more difficult if screws are used for mounting. Circular bull's-eye levels are too small to be installed accurately and are hard to interpret. The large curved levels that are made of 1-inch-diameter clear tubing and designed to be mounted on the front of a trailer are satisfactory for side-to-side leveling.

We use a good-quality, 9-inch-long torpedo level; this length is more than accurate enough for any RV leveling. The bubble rests between two heavy lines when the RV is level. If one end of the bubble abuts the lighter lines slightly to the left or right of the heavier lines, the RV will be about 2 degrees off level; this is satisfactory for operating most brands of older refrigerators.

To level a trailer from front to back, raise or lower the tongue jack on a conventional trailer, or the two front jacks on a fifth-wheel. To be leveled in this direction, a self-propelled RV needs to have levelers under both front or both back wheels. In some situations, one wheel of a motorhome may need levelers for fore-and-aft as well as levelers for side-to-side.

If the site surface is grass or dirt, put a board under any jack so it won't sink into the ground if it rains. We carry small, thin boards just for this purpose. Most automatic levelers have good-size pads, but they too should have a board larger than the pad under them in sites where the surface is, or may become, soft.

Levelers can be just about anything that elevate the RV's wheels and support its weight. They can be purchased or you can make your own.

Figure 8-3. *A combination of 2 x 8 and ½-inch plywood boards is used to level this trailer.*

We use four 2 x 8 boards, two of which are slightly shorter than the others. The ends are cut on a 45-degree angle so the tires won't run up over a sharp edge. We also have six ½-inch-thick plywood boards, 6 inches wide by 13 inches long. If two of these under each wheel don't do the job, they can be used in various combinations with the 2 x 8 boards (Figure 8-3).

We have seen homemade ramps made of graduated 2 x 4s nailed together, one on top of another (Figure 8-4). A 2 x 4 is narrower than the tire tread on many RVs and therefore not wide enough to fully support the tires (boards used for leveling should always be wider than the tread). This type of ramp offers little flexibility for leveling adjustments, and is heavy, unwieldy, and may be difficult to store.

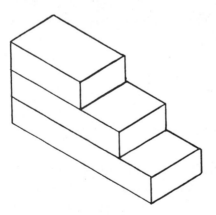

Figure 8-4. *Stacked 2 x 4s attached to one another are difficult to store and do not provide a support wide enough for tires.*

Many RVs have an outside locker where short, loose boards can be stored conveniently. If the boards and the level are accessible and easy to use, leveling can be accomplished quickly.

When using boards, the actual process of leveling is nothing more than judging how much height is needed and placing the appropriate number of boards in front of (or behind) the wheels, then pulling forward (or backing) onto them. After leveling your RV a few times, you will have a good idea of how much height is needed and selecting the proper boards will become second nature.

If our trailer's wheels are propped up rather high, or if the site has a fore-and-aft slope to it, we always put chocks against the wheels on the unraised side of the trailer. Wheel chocks can be homemade or purchased; suitable rocks or logs at the site can also be used.

The Hookups and Related Systems

A full-hookup site has water, electricity, and a sewer drain. Some campgrounds have sites with water and electricity but no sewer drain; in this case, holding tanks are emptied at the campground's dump station.

The equipment needed for using the hookups consists of a shore-power cable, water and sewer hoses, and various accessories. RVs are equipped with a built-in shore-power cable and many come with a sewer hose; the RVer is responsible for supplying the water hose and the accessories.

The RV should be placed in the site so the shore-power cable reaches the electrical outlet, the water hose reaches the faucet, and the sewer hose reaches the sewer drain. If in doubt about whether the shore-power cable can reach the outlet—before leveling the RV and proceeding with setting up—pull out the cable to see if it is long enough. If it's just a few feet short, back up or pull forward until it reaches the outlet. (If it is still too short, an extension is needed.) Use the same procedure if you are unsure about the sewer hose extending to the drain.

If your RV has louvered windows, keep them closed while setting up. The sharp corners are hazardous when you walk around the RV or, after stooping, when you stand up under an open window.

Water Hookup Equipment

For clean, safe water, the hose you use should be made of a nontoxic material. Keep such a hose in the RV and use it only for the water supply; don't just toss in the garden hose before leaving on a trip. The packaging should stipulate that the hose is safe for drinking water. Green hoses sold in garden shops are not suitable; white and blue hoses, and certain reel-type hoses, are for potable water and labeled accordingly. These hoses are sold in RV and marine supply stores and some hardware stores.

Drinking-water hoses are either round or flat; we've used both types and much prefer a flat hose. It drains rapidly because it doesn't curl up, it can be folded quickly, and it takes up much less storage space than a coiled, round hose of the same length. Flat hoses are not as common as round ones, but they can be special-ordered from most RV supply stores.

A reel hose is flat and stores neatly in its own case, but it has drawbacks. To use it, the entire hose must be removed from the reel. The hose must be completely free of kinks, but because it is made of fabric, laying it flat can be difficult. Squeegee rollers drain the hose as it is rewound, but if the rollers do not work properly, it is impossible to put all the hose back on the reel. Kinks also must be avoided when rewinding.

Drinking-water hoses come in 25- and 50-foot lengths. We have found a 50-footer to be the most practical; a 25-foot hose is often too short because in some campsites, the water faucet isn't convenient to the RV's city-water connection or to the fill pipe for the internal tank.

For easier handling and draining, we cut our 50-foot hose into 30- and 20-foot lengths, and added appropriate fittings to the ends. The short hose is used when the water hookup is nearby; the long hose is used alone or added to the short section when the water supply is farther away.

A few low-cost accessories enable you to safely and conveniently use all the various types of campground water hookups. The most important accessory is a water-pressure regulator (Figure 8-5). City water may be delivered at an extremely high pressure, which can rupture hoses and the plastic plumbing in an RV. A regulator holds the pressure to 45 pounds per square inch. Some regulators have a dial meter so the actual pressure can be read.

A "Y" shut-off valve is handy when one faucet serves two campsites. A 90-degree connector, or water-entry elbow, allows the hose to hang vertically, eliminating the kink that occurs when a hose is

Figure 8-5. *A water-pressure regulator maintains city water at a pressure that should not harm an RV's plumbing.* (Courtesy Marshall Brass Company)

inserted directly into the fill pipe of the internal tank or attached to the city-water connection.

In public campgrounds, one water faucet may be centrally located to service several sites. The faucet usually does not have threads for attaching a hose to discourage campers from hooking up to the communal spigot. If you need to attach a hose to the faucet temporarily—to fill your water tank, for example—a product called a Water Thief can be used. This is nothing more than a male hose connection on the end of a short rubber sleeve with gripping rings inside, which is slipped onto the unthreaded faucet. Another useful accessory is a regular, adjustable hose nozzle.

The Water Hookup

In most campgrounds, hookups are located on the left side of the site (the street side of the RV). The water hookup is usually near the electric hookup, but it may be at the rear of the site. If it is between two adjacent sites, the water for one RV is on the right side of the site.

In many campgrounds, the faucet is atop a pipe that may be a couple of inches to a foot or two above the ground. Sometimes the water connection is in a frost-proof box or another type of enclosure. If the campground is located where severe winter weather occurs, the faucet may be on a pipe about 4 feet above the ground and have a handle that is raised (rather than a knob that is turned), to start the flow of water; the valve is in the ground below the frost line.

Hooking up the water involves nothing more than attaching one end of the hose to the faucet and the other to the city-water connection on the RV. If a water-pressure regulator is used, attach it to the faucet end to protect the hose from rupturing.

Most RVers hook up to city water when it's available, but we do not. We always use water from the internal tank, no matter how long we stay in one place. Constantly replenishing the supply assures us of clean, fresh water, and we can camp in places without hookups (which we often do) without taking any special measures to ready the water supply.

Furthermore, if an RV is hooked up to city water and a leak develops in the plumbing, water will flow until it is turned off at the outside faucet. On more than one occasion we've noticed water dripping from the underside of an RV parked next to us. In all instances, the occupants of the RV were unaware of the leak until we told them.

If we did hook up to city water, we would always turn off the water at the faucet whenever leaving the trailer. Most RVers don't do this; in fact, we have seen only one RVer who did: A permanent campground resident always turned off the faucet before he left for work and turned it on when he came back. We assume he started the practice after a leak occurred when he was away.

Leaks also can develop when using the internal tank, so we make it a practice to turn off the water pump switch when we leave the trailer for a time. If you are using city water and you notice water coming from the base of the toilet, it may be because the pressure is too great.

We don't believe a water treatment system is necessary for RVs, but we do want our water to be filtered. We use a filter with a replaceable charcoal cartridge that removes odors, sediment, and chlorine taste (Figure 8-6).

Even with a filter, we check any water we think may be questionable before putting it in our tank by running some into a clear glass. If nothing is floating in it, we taste a sample. We won't put water with a bad taste or visible impurities in our tank. If water is rusty, running it for a while usually clears it up.

In some parts of the country, water has a sulfurous odor. We have no qualms about using this water because we have found that the aeration it receives while sloshing in the tank when the RV is moving removes the smell. When your RV is hooked up to sulfurous city water, however, the water won't have the benefit of aeration.

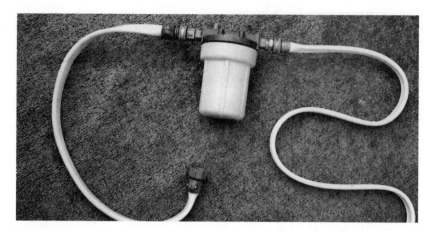

Figure 8-6. *The authors' water filter with replaceable charcoal cartridges that remove sediment and objectionable tastes from water. Because this filter is designed for permanent installation in a water line, it was modified to accept hose fittings.*

If you use an in-line filter, install it close to the hookup faucet so the filtering begins at the water source.

When the hose is drained and ready for storage, screw the ends together to keep insects and dirt out, and any water remaining in the hose from leaking into the storage compartment.

To prevent the hose from snaking around in its storage place, keep it in a bag made of sturdy plastic or fabric. We keep all hose accessories and a spare filter cartridge together in a plastic container in the hose storage compartment.

Sewer Hookup Equipment

To empty holding tanks, a sewer hose with appropriate fittings on each end is needed. Sewer hoses are 3 inches in diameter and made of vinyl reinforced with a spiral-wound wire along the entire length. Some hoses are extremely flexible and can be stretched considerably beyond their collapsed length; they are blue or brown in color. A more rigid type, which collapses only a little, is black or dark green, and made of tougher material that lasts much longer than flexible hoses.

All sewer hoses are available in 10-foot lengths; the blue and brown hoses are also available in 20-foot lengths. Two hoses of any type can be joined together with a coupler.

A sewer hose can't be used without an adapter on one end that attaches to the RV's sewer-pipe hose-connection fitting, and it should have another fitting on the other end that is placed in the campground drain. Two bayonet hooks on the adapter engage small knobs on the hose-connection fitting. The drain fitting, usually a coupler that protrudes from the end of the hose, helps to hold the hose in the drain; this fitting is also used to join two lengths of hose.

The dealer may provide a sewer hose with a new RV, but you will probably have to install the fittings yourself; this is not difficult. You will need hot water, two stainless steel hose clamps large enough to fit around the hose, and a screwdriver to tighten the clamps. Pour the hot water on the hose end to expand it, then slip the fitting for either end inside the hose and tighten the clamp over the area where the fitting extends inside. Be sure the clamp is flat against the hose and not canted. It should be tight, but, if snugged down too much, the clamp edges may cut into the flexible-type hose, creating a hole, and thus a leak. The clamp holds the fitting in place and prevents sewage from leaking around it. This method is also used to install a coupler. A hose clamp should be on each side of a coupler when it's used to join two hoses together.

Some fittings are threaded and can be screwed into the hose. Hot water is not necessary for installation, but coating the end of the fitting with liquid soap makes the insertion easier. To prevent leaks, use a hose clamp on this type of fitting. Threaded fittings have a drain arrangement different than other types: The drain-end fitting is angled at 90 degrees and fits into a separate accessory with a flanged section on top of a short, 3-inch-diameter pipe. The pipe is put into the drain and the wide flange holds it securely in place. To store the sewer hose in its compartment, the flange has to be removed.

Some sewer hoses can be purchased with sizing rings in each end; an adapter is installed simply by slipping it in.

In some campgrounds, local regulations require the use of a special screw-type drain fitting; if so, the fittings are for sale in the campground store or office. The fitting is not expensive, but for an overnight stay it is a nuisance to change it to the required one and then change back to a standard fitting the next morning. If you stay in such a campground, perhaps you can delay emptying the holding tanks to avoid changing the fitting.

A trailer's sewer hose is typically stored in the back bumper, but some units have a PVC pipe attached to the underbody to hold the hose. Many newer motorhomes have a separate compartment where the holding-tank valves are located and the hose is stored. If your RV has no special place for a hose (which is unlikely), don't put it into any storage compartment without first placing it in a sturdy plastic bag. We observed one RVer who, immediately after dumping his waste, tossed the still-dripping sewer hose into the same compartment with his water hose—a bad practice!

The Sewer Hookup

Sewer drains are usually on the left side of the site, although they are occasionally at the rear. In older campgrounds and some mobile home parks with sites set aside for RVs, the sewer drain may be in the middle of the site. Such a drain ends up under an RV when it is parked, making the sewer connection difficult.

If the campground manager doesn't accompany you to the site and show you where all the hookups are located, you will have to find them yourself. The water faucet and electrical outlet are usually obvious, but the sewer opening may be concealed by high grass or covered with leaves. If it's not visible, look around the site for a cap or metal plate that may be the cover for the drain, being careful not to step into an uncovered drain.

Emptying the Holding Tanks

The dumping procedure for the holding tanks is as follows: Be sure both gate valves are closed. Remove the cap from the RV's sewer pipe. (The cap has bayonet hooks like those on the hose adapter and a strap that keeps it connected to the pipe.) Attach the end of the hose with the adapter to the sewer-pipe hose-connection fitting. Extend the hose and place it well down in the drain. Open the gate valve to the tank you want to drain. If you need to dump both tanks when you arrive at a campground (or a dump station), empty the black water first so the gray water flushes out any solids remaining in the hose. Chapter 4 explains the order in which valves should be kept open when staying for a while in a site with a sewer hookup.

Standard 10-foot sewer hoses are more than long enough to reach most sewer drains, so they often lie on the ground in loops. To completely drain the hose, pick it up at various points along its length, starting at the end connected to the RV, so all the waste runs through; be careful not to pull the drain end out while doing so.

The hose won't have to be lifted for draining if it rests on a slanted ramp. Some RVers make a ramp of 2 x 4s or use one that is ready-made (available at RV supply stores). Manufactured sewer-hose supports are either a solid plastic, U-shaped type that telescopes, or the type that extends to support the hose at many points along its length and compresses for convenient storage.

Sewer Dumping Practices.   When we handle any dumping equipment, we always wear rubber gloves: for connecting, disconnecting, and handling the sewer hose; for removing the cap on the drain opening at a dump station or campground site; for opening and closing the holding-tank valves; and for removing and replacing the cap on the RV's sewer pipe. We like the type of heavy-duty gloves used by commercial fishermen and farmers because they are loose-fitting and can be slipped on and off easily. We don't touch anything with the gloves except sewage-related items. Once the dumping is done, the gloves are rinsed with fresh water. If only a potable-water faucet is available for rinsing, such as at a campground site, the gloves are not allowed to touch the faucet. They are stored in a plastic bag to prevent contact with other items in the compartment where they are kept.

After the dumping is done, as you prepare to leave a campsite, make sure the holding-tank valves are closed all the way. Then disconnect the hose from the RV's sewer pipe, using one hand to hold up the end of the hose so nothing can spill out, and the other hand to replace the cap on the pipe. (If the cap is replaced immediately after removing the hose, it's unlikely that you will forget to put it on—we've seen many RVs on the highway with the sewer cap dangling.) Next, walk toward the drain holding the hose elevated so any residue runs into the drain. If the site's water faucet is nearby, the hose should be flushed with water before stowing it. Keep the hose end well away from the faucet—never allow sewer equipment to touch any part of a potable-water supply. When we flush the hose this way, we remove one glove before touching the faucet.

After both gate valves are tightly closed, a little waste may remain in the RV's pipe and spill out when the hose is removed (it will be gray water if the tanks were emptied in the proper order). If the RV is parked on a paved site, the water hose or a bucket of water should be used to rinse away any spillage. It is our practice to flush any spillage with water, even when the RV is parked in a grass or gravel site.

When stowing the sewer hose in a bumper, put the drain end in first so the adapter end will be just inside the opening. Most bumpers are barely large enough to accommodate the adapter; it may need to be wiggled or pushed in with some force (and it may take some effort to remove it). A sewer hose lasts longer if it isn't dragged across abrasive materials, such as concrete or gravel.

Dump Station Procedures. There are times when a dump station must be used rather than a campsite sewer. A well-designed dump station has a drain in the center of a sloping concrete apron and a faucet with a hose attached for rinsing the apron (Figure 8-7). Some dump stations also have a potable-water faucet for filling the RV's water tank. A potable-water faucet should be labeled as such. Although a hose may be connected to the faucet, we always use our own hose to fill the tank—our practice ever since we saw an RVer put a well-labeled potable-water hose down her toilet to rinse out the holding tank.

The procedure for emptying holding tanks at a dump station is exactly the same as at a campsite sewer, but, remarkable as it seems, some people don't use a sewer hose at a dump station. We suspect these bad-mannered people know the proper method for disposing of their waste but don't use it because it takes too long to do it the right way, or, more likely, they can simply drive away from their mess, leaving it for someone else to clean up. Maybe we are wrong, however; perhaps some RVers don't know that a sewer hose should always be used for dumping. Without a hose, the stream of sewage spewing from the RV's pipe can't possibly enter the hose-size drain of the dump station. If the drain opening is flush with the apron, some of the liquid sewage runs into drain, but most of the toilet tissue and fecal matter remains on the apron. Inconsiderate RVers who use this dumping procedure are unlikely to use available water to rinse the apron.

Unfortunately, bad dumping practices are not uncommon. When emptying sewage into a campsite drain or at a dump station, be sure you practice good RVing etiquette.

Other Methods of Waste Disposal. Public campgrounds without sewer hookups may have a gray-water drain at each site or one

Figure 8-7. *This well-designed dump station has the drain in a sloping apron.*

drain for several sites. Gray water is collected in a bucket or another container and carried to the drain for disposal. Using a sewer hose to dispose of gray water in this type of drain is usually not allowed because some people would certainly take advantage of the situation and try to dump the contents of their black-water tank. Dumping gray water with a garden hose, however, may be permitted.

To facilitate dumping in these circumstances, we replaced the standard cap on our trailer's sewer pipe with a cap that has a threaded water-hose connection. For use, the covering on the hose connection is removed and a garden hose is attached to the cap. The hose is placed in the drain (often basin-shaped and about 2 feet high), then the gray-water valve is opened. After the tank is drained, the valve is closed and the hose removed; the hose shouldn't be left in the drain. We use an inexpensive green garden hose for gray-water dumping; it can never be mistaken for our white drinking-water hose.

RVers who have tent trailers or pickup campers without holding tanks have to dispose of gray water by collecting it in a container or, in sites with a sewer, attaching a garden hose to the sink drain hose and running it to the sewer.

When staying for some time in a campground that has a dump station but no sewer hookups at the sites, a portable holding tank can be used instead of periodically moving the RV to the dump station. Portable tanks are made of sturdy plastic; have a large, capped drain opening; and can be used for both gray and black water. Capacities range from 5 to 22 gallons, and all but the 5-gallon size have wheels so they can be easily trundled to a dump station. To facilitate emptying, a short sewer hose that attaches to the tank's drain opening is available.

Some RVs have portable toilets. They can be emptied at a dump station or at a specific facility some campgrounds have designated for this purpose. Emptying the waste into a regular toilet is not permitted in most campgrounds; check with the management before dumping in this manner. If you do use a regular toilet, empty the waste in several stages, flushing between each—don't dump it in all at once.

Electric Hookup Equipment

An RV's 120-volt shore-power cable is compatible with most campground electrical outlets, but RVers should carry a few accessories for easy and convenient hooking up and, more importantly, for determining

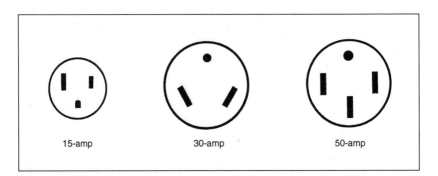

15-amp   30-amp   50-amp

Figure 8-8. *Campground outlet configurations. The 30-amp outlet is the most common.*

whether the campsite's electricity is safe to use.

RVers who do considerable traveling will encounter electrical receptacles with different types of configurations (Figure 8-8). Most RVs have a shore-power cable with a 30-amp plug that has two large, flat blades and one round or U-shaped pin, which fits into a 30-amp receptacle. Recently constructed or remodeled campgrounds with electric hookups generally have outlets with a 30-amp receptacle at each site. Outlets in older campgrounds may be the 15-amp type, which accept

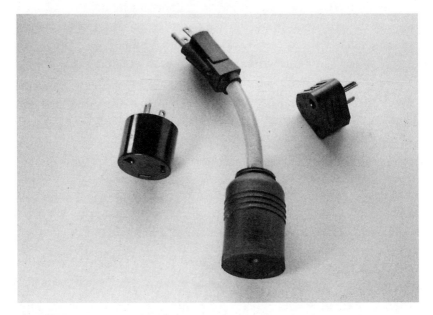

Figure 8-9. *Various types of 15-amp male/30-amp female adapters.*

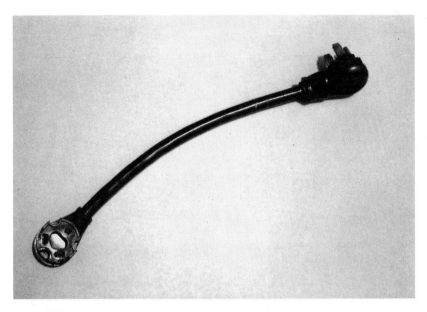

Figure 8-10. *A 50-amp male/30-amp female adapter.*

the common household plug with two flat, parallel blades (smaller than those on 30-amp plugs) and a round or U-shaped pin.

Many large motorhomes are wired for 50-amp, 240-volt service, and some newer campgrounds have receptacles that accommodate these RVs. A 50-amp plug has three large, flat, parallel blades and a round pin.

Any campground outlet with a 50-amp receptacle probably also has a 30-amp receptacle, and may even have a 15-amp receptacle; in mobile home parks with RV sites, the only electric hookup may be a 50-amp receptacle.

To plug into each type of receptacle, adapters are needed. As full-timers, we carry many adapters, but the one that we use the most and that RVers should include in their electrical equipment is a 15-amp male/30-amp female adapter (Figure 8-9). This adapter allows the shore-power cable with its 30-amp plug to be used in a 15-amp receptacle. We also carry a 50-amp male/30-amp female adapter to use in 50-amp receptacles (Figure 8-10).

If an RV is equipped for 50-amp service, an adapter is needed to use the four-prong, 50-amp plug on the shore-power cable in 30- and 15-amp receptacles. A 30-amp receptacle requires a 30-amp male/50-amp

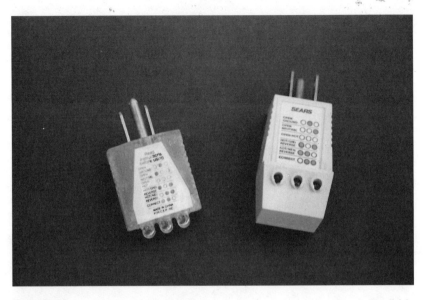

Figure 8-11. *A circuit analyzer (two common types are shown here) should be used to determine whether campground outlets are safe to use.*

female adapter, and a 15-amp male/50-amp female adapter is needed for a 15-amp receptacle.

A 25- or 50-foot extension cord can be useful. In older public campgrounds, the electrical outlet may be a considerable distance from the site; we also have stayed in private campgrounds where an extension cord was necessary. Ideally, the extension cord should be the heavy-duty type designated "10/3" (the figures are usually imprinted at intervals along the cord). This designation means that the cord is composed of three 10-gauge wires. This size is suitable for carrying most RV loads; a 12/3 cord can be used if high-wattage items are used sparingly. An extension cord designated 14/3 or 16/3 has a wire gauge too light for safe RV use. (In wire-gauge designations, the higher the number, the lighter the wire, and vice versa.) An extension cord has a 15-amp plug. To plug it into a 30-amp outlet, a 30-amp male/15-amp female adapter is needed.

An accessory no RVer should be without is a circuit analyzer (Figure 8-11). It indicates if an outlet is properly wired and safe to use. Although it is rare to find a seriously unsafe electrical condition, checking out an outlet requires only this inexpensive ($10 or less) accessory and no special skills.

A circuit analyzer has the familiar 15-amp, three-prong plug on one end and three small lights on the other. It is simply plugged into a receptacle to get the status of the circuit. For use in a 30-amp receptacle, plug a 30-amp male/15-amp female adapter into the outlet, and the circuit analyzer into the adapter.

Once the analyzer is plugged in, the configuration of the illuminated lights indicates one of five circuit conditions in the outlet: correct wiring, reversed polarity, open neutral, open ground, or hot and ground reversed. Of course, if no lights are lit, the outlet has no power. The code for interpreting the indicator lights is printed on the analyzer.

If the circuit analyzer indicates any condition other than correct, inform the campground management and move to another site. *If the analyzer shows that the hot and ground wires are reversed, never, under any circumstances, use the electricity.* You are in danger of a lethal electrical shock if the shore-power cable is plugged in and you touch the metal skin or any other metal on or connected to the RV. Be extra careful when removing the circuit analyzer from the outlet because the same shock hazard exists if the outlet's metal box is touched. This condition is described first because it is the most dangerous of all wiring abnormalities; however, it is also the least frequently encountered.

A shock hazard can also exist when the circuit analyzer shows an open ground; a GFCI doesn't provide its protective function without a good ground. In this case, a shock can occur if a defective electrical appliance or tool is used.

Reversed polarity is not dangerous to an RV's occupants, but operating a TV and other electronic equipment on a circuit with reversed polarity can damage this equipment.

When the circuit analyzer indicates an open neutral, the outlet usually doesn't provide usable power to the RV; it can be considered dead, although power is still present.

After reading about all the things that can be wrong with electrical outlets, understand that most campground outlets are wired correctly. If your circuit analyzer indicates a problem, however, most campground managers will assign you to another site.

A normal campground outlet should provide 120-volt service, the same voltage supplied to residences, but sometimes the voltage is lower (the reasons are explained later in this chapter). Knowing the voltage is useful because it is neither safe nor sensible to operate the RV's electrical equipment when the voltage is lower than 105 volts. Low voltage can damage some equipment; furthermore, operating high-wattage equipment on voltage that is too low may cause a fire. A voltage meter, another low-cost, easy-to-use accessory, indicates the amount of voltage coming into the RV.

The simplest, most convenient voltage meter to use is the type that plugs into a 15-amp receptacle. Because voltage can fluctuate, after using the meter for an initial voltage check on the site's electrical outlet (use the appropriate adapter, if necessary), it should be plugged into a receptacle inside the RV for continuous monitoring of the voltage.

Some more expensive circuit analyzers also have a voltage readout, but certain models of this type have only two lights instead of three, indicating just four wiring conditions. A two-light analyzer does not show the dangerous condition of hot and ground wire reversal. If you have a two-light analyzer/voltage meter, it can be used for monitoring, but use a three-light analyzer for the initial outlet check.

Because we make a circuit-analyzer check on every outlet we use, we want a convenient method for doing so. Part of our getting-under-way routine includes plugging a circuit analyzer into an under-cabinet receptacle in the galley, where it is visible from the outside through the window. Because the galley is on the street side (as are most campsite hookups), when we next plug in, a glance in the window tells us the status of the outlet's wiring.

If an outlet looks old or burned, or if we suspect something else is wrong with it, before pulling into the site—especially if it's difficult to get into—we check the outlet with another circuit analyzer kept handy in the shore-power cable compartment. At times, we also check the voltage before getting situated in a site.

The Electric Hookup

Campground electric hookups run the gamut from old-fashioned, exposed-to-the-weather, fused, 15-amp receptacles attached to anything handy at the site—a pole, a stake, a tree—to modern, covered electrical boxes containing circuit breakers and a combination of 50-, 30-, and 15-amp receptacles. The rather haphazard, makeshift electric hookups are mostly encountered in older campgrounds, especially in some city, county, and state parks, but most campgrounds have proper electric hookups.

Ideally, the electrical outlet is on the left side of the site near the middle or toward the rear of the RV, but in some campgrounds it is at the front of the site or far to the rear. The outlet may not be obvious; if you haven't been shown its location, look on the back side of posts or trees at the site or inside any enclosure. An enclosed outlet may be in a wooden box, but more often it is in a gray or green metal box.

Before plugging in, check the outlet with a circuit analyzer for the conditions discussed previously. If the analyzer shows anything but a correct circuit, do not use the electricity. If the circuit is okay, the shore-power cable can be plugged in; use the appropriate adapter, if necessary.

If the circuit analyzer indicates no power (no lights lit), check whether the circuit breaker for the receptacle is on. When there is more than one receptacle in a metal box, the circuit breakers are usually inside the box, to the side of or below the receptacles. Few campground outlets are fused anymore; if they exist, they are the 15-amp type. When the outlet has a screw-type fuse instead of a circuit breaker, check to see that a fuse is in the socket, that it is screwed in all the way, and that it has not blown. Also make sure the plug prongs of the shore-power cable are inserted all the way into the receptacle. If there is still no power, inform the campground manager.

When the shore-power cable is plugged into an operative outlet but the RV is not receiving power, be sure the main breaker and other circuit breakers in the RV's system are on. If there is power everywhere except in one RV circuit, check the fuse or breaker for that circuit.

The next step should be to check the voltage. In newer campgrounds, which should have proper wiring, a voltage check isn't absolutely necessary, but in older campgrounds where wiring is suspect, you should know the voltage to decide which electrical equipment you can use. Unfortunately, if the campground is inadequately wired and other RVers are using high-wattage equipment, voltage may be low, and moving to another site won't necessarily improve the situation because all sites will have the same condition. If you stay at an older campground, be careful about the load you put on the circuit; it may preclude using an air conditioner or electric heater.

Sometimes when low voltage exists, it's not the fault of the campground's system; using an extension cord of unsuitably sized wire gauge can cause low voltage.

After setting up, put a voltage meter in an interior receptacle to monitor voltage during your stay.

Campground Wiring

This section is not a highly technical discussion about electricity, but you should know something about the wiring in campgrounds to understand how the RV can be affected by the electricity supplied.

Amperage is the numerical value of current, and voltage is the "force" behind the current. The force is referred to as a potential— meaning the electricity at a campground outlet has the potential to deliver 120 volts. Except for unusual circumstances (such as brownouts), the potential—120 volts—is delivered.

Wire is rated by the amount of amperage it can safely carry. The ease with which current can flow through a wire depends on the wire's size and length. Just as a water hose can carry a flow of water up to a certain pressure before it bursts, a wire of a given size can carry only a certain amount of current (amperage) before it overheats and burns. To continue the hose analogy for voltage: In a 100-foot hose, the pressure of the flowing water is less at the end of the hose than at the faucet. The same is true in an electric wire: The voltage (pressure) at the outlet is 120 volts, but it can drop progressively along a long length of wire if the wire isn't heavy enough. For a simplistic example: If a campground is wired with undersized wire, in a row of campsites the sites nearest the source of electricity may receive the full 120 volts; those in the middle, perhaps 117 volts; and those on the end, maybe only 113 volts. When the campground is properly wired (as most are), the full 120-volt potential is available at each outlet, but voltage may be reduced if RVers in other sites are using heaters, air conditioners, and other high-wattage equipment. The combination of inadequate wiring and overloading can cause the voltage at sites on the end of the circuit to drop to an unsafe level. Electrical equipment damage can occur and fire hazards exist when voltage is too low.

Living Within the Available Amperage

To avoid overloading problems, RVers should learn to live within the amperage available from the campground outlet. This is not too difficult with the 100 amps available with 240-volt service (two 120-volt legs of 50 amps each), and even 30-amp service is not too restrictive, but with only 15 amps available, electricity must be used judiciously.

It is important to know the wattage or amperage draw for all AC electrical equipment in the RV (Table 8-1, page 168). This information is on the case or cover of each item, or in the instruction manual. Most electrical appliances have ratings in watts, which is converted into amperage by dividing the wattage by the voltage (120 volts). An item rated at 1,500 watts (a common wattage of electric heaters) draws 12.5 amps (1,500 divided by 120 equals 12.5). When the amperage ratings are known, it's easy to mentally add the amperages of equipment that will be in use at the same time. If the total is higher than the service provided from the campground outlet, some items will have to be turned off while others are in use to avoid tripping a circuit breaker or blowing a fuse. It takes some mental adjustment from the way you operate at home; for instance, in your RV you may not be able to use the toaster and coffeemaker at the same time (brew the coffee first; it won't cool much as you make the toast). Depending on the amperage available, it may be necessary to turn off an electric heater when the microwave oven is in use (cooking is quick in a microwave, so the heater won't be off long).

Equipment that is constantly running is often overlooked in amperage calculations. A 6-cubic-foot absorption-type refrigerator operating on AC power uses 2.7 amps; a 40-amp converter/charger consumes about 1 amp when operating at minimum load (when charging a seriously depleted battery, it operates at full load: 5.5 amps). Combined, these loads total almost 4 amps (not including any other equipment that may be in use). Adding a 13,500-Btu air conditioner that requires 13.6 amps, or a 1,500-watt heater drawing 12.5 amps, pushes consumption above what a 15-amp circuit can safely carry continuously. It may be possible to use these items at the same time because they all cycle during operation and do not run constantly at maximum amperage load. If you experience repeated circuit-breaker tripping at the campground outlet, however, it's almost certainly because the circuit is overloaded.

Electric heaters and air conditioners cause most of the problems with 15-amp campground hookups, but with improper use of any high-wattage appliances, an outlet's receptacle contacts can burn, possibly

Table 8-1. Wattage and Amperage of AC Appliances

Appliance	Watts	Amps
TV, color, 9-inch, AC or AC/DC	54	0.45
TV, color, 13-inch, AC or AC/DC	70	0.58
TV satellite and receiver	170	1.41
Videocassette recorder (VCR)	90	0.75
Videocassette player (VCP), AC/DC on AC	18	0.15
Refrigerator, 6-cubic-foot, AC/gas, on AC	300	2.70
Refrigerator, 8-cubic-foot, AC/gas, on AC	300	2.70
Refrigerator, portable, AC/DC, on AC	47	0.39
Converter/charger, 20-amp, at maximum rating	420	3.50
Converter/charger, 30-amp, at maximum rating	552	4.60
Converter/charger, 40-amp, at maximum rating	660	5.50
Converter/charger, 75-amp, at maximum rating	1,040	8.66
Air conditioner, 14,800-Btu/hr.	1,920	16.00
Air conditioner, 13,500-Btu/hr.	1,700	14.16
Air conditioner, 7,100-Btu/hr.	1,200	10.00
Air conditioner, heat strip	1,920	16.00
Heater, electric	1,500	12.50
Heater, electric, on 1,250-watt setting	1,250	10.41
Microwave oven, small, 450-watt cooking rating	900	7.50
Microwave oven, large, 650-watt cooking rating	1,300	10.83
Coffeemaker	900	7.50
Iron	1,300	10.83
Hair dryer	1,200	10.00
Blender	300	2.50
Toaster	900	7.50
Vacuum, canister	350	2.91
Vacuum, hand	240	2.00
Computer, desktop	100	0.83
Computer printer	240	2.00
Drill, ⅜-inch	350	2.90
Saber saw	300	2.50

Note:

These ratings are approximate, and may vary among manufacturers and from product to product.

resulting in a fire, and the campground circuit can become so over-loaded that the voltage drops to an unsafe level. Repeated overloading also hastens the burning of the shore-power cable plug.

The size of an adapter governs the amount of amperage available. For example, if a 30-amp shore-power cable is plugged into a 15-amp male/30-amp female adapter for use in a 15-amp outlet, 15 amps is all that can be safely used.

The Cable TV Connection

Cable TV is available in many private campgrounds where regular reception is not good, and may even be offered in campgrounds in or near metropolitan areas where reception is excellent.

Many RVs built in recent years have an exterior cable TV connection, usually on the street side in a small box with a lift-up lid. (There may be an adjoining box with an outlet connection so a TV can be used outdoors with either the cable or antenna system.)

For viewing cable channels, the TV should be the cable-ready type (the instruction manual describes the TV as "cable-ready" or "cable-compatible"). TVs smaller than those with a 9-inch screen don't have the cable-ready feature. Some cable channels can be received on non-compatible TVs, but only up to Channel 13, unless a converter box is used.

A length of cable with the appropriate F-style fittings on each end is needed for a cable hookup. Sometimes this is provided by the campground, but if you don't want to be without cable TV when it's available, you should have your own cable. A 25-foot TV coaxial extension (available wherever TV accessories are sold) is not expensive, and is usually more than long enough. You will need the round 75-ohm type, not the flat-ribbon 300-ohm type.

The cable hookup at the campsite is rather obvious if a short length of cable is visible on a post, but sometimes it can be hard to locate. If so, inspect any boxes at the site; we have occasionally found the tiny connection mounted on the underside of the electric box. You can also look at other RVs to determine where the cable hookup is located.

If your RV doesn't have an exterior cable connection, the cable has to be routed to the interior and connected directly to the TV. Routing the cable through an entry door or window isn't the best arrangement; the door may not close properly and the window has to be open a crack with the cable somehow routed through the screen. If your RV has an outside compartment that is open to the inside of the RV, routing the cable through it may be feasible.

Setting-up Procedures

Everyone develops a routine for setting up camp, but placing the RV in the site so the hookups are reachable and leveling the RV should be done first. After that, setting-up duties can be taken care of in any order. Here's a list of what we must do to set up camp with our fifth-wheel trailer:

• Situate trailer in site.

• Level side-to-side and chock wheels.

• Lower front jacks.

• Unhitch and move truck forward.

• Level fore and aft.

• Connect to the electric hookup.

• Connect sewer hose, if necessary.

• Lower rear stabilizing jacks.

• Set up front stabilizing jack.

• Raise stone shields.

• Turn on propane cylinders.

• Light water heater.

• Raise TV antenna or make cable connection.

After the fore-and-aft leveling, the other duties are not done in any particular order; we do them as they are convenient. The entire setting-up procedure takes us about 15 to 20 minutes.

No matter what type of RV you have, setting up should be as simple as setting up our fifth-wheel trailer. After going through the routine a few times, you shouldn't need more than 15 to 20 minutes to set up. A possible exception is if you have a tent trailer; the unfolding and securing of the trailer itself can take a little longer.

Inside, there should be little to do other than turn on the refrigerator and set in place items, such as the TV, that were stowed for traveling. Depending on the weather, the furnace or air conditioner may have to be turned on.

Some couples share the setting-up duties, as we do, or just one may do the entire job. Children who are old enough may enjoy having specific duties to perform after arriving at a campsite.

Stone Shields

The main purpose of a trailer's front stone shield is to protect windows from stones and flying debris thrown up by the wheels of the tow vehicle while the trailer is moving. When the trailer is parked, the stone shield provides shade and keeps rain from coming into open windows. Some RVers place stone shields at angles that are worthless for either purpose. A stone shield should be angled slightly downward, not straight out or upward.

Some stone shields have a gas-strut lifting mechanism that puts the shield at the same level every time it is raised, but most have a sliding support that is held in place by tightening a wing nut. Because each side is adjusted independently, it can be difficult to raise the sides equally. To overcome this, after we purchased our trailer, the shield was raised to the proper angle and the sides adjusted equally. With a permanent marker, a line was drawn on each support under the sliding portion. Now, when the bottom of the sliding portion is on the mark, the stone shield is perfectly adjusted. If your RV has an awning, make sure it is raised high enough to clear the entry door when the door is opened.

Jacks

RV occupants are more comfortable if stabilizing jacks are used to steady the unit so it won't bounce and rock. Some RVs have built-in stabilizing jacks that are manually raised and lowered by a handle. Other portable stabilizing jacks have a pyramid-shaped base into which a threaded post is inserted; the post is raised or lowered by turning an adjusting slip-rod. The built-in type is the easiest to use because the handle is operated while you are standing at the side of the unit. The other type requires getting down on hands and knees to place the jacks under the RV and adjust the post to the correct height. Some motorhomes are equipped with automatic levelers, which also serve as stabilizers.

A portable jack should always be placed so the top rests against a chassis member and propped up, if necessary, to make it sit straight; a crooked jack can pop out. If the jacks aren't on a paved surface, place a pad, such as a piece of ½-inch plywood, under the base. Built-in jacks should also be on pads when they rest on an unpaved surface.

Portable jacks are sometimes referred to as "stacker jacks" because when the posts are removed, the bases nest, or stack, one inside the other for compact storage.

Conventional and tent trailers should have four stabilizing jacks, two on each side at the front and the rear. Self-propelled RVs with the engine in front may need only rear jacks because the weight of the engine tends to keep the front steady. For diesel-pusher motorhomes, where the engine is in the rear, the reverse applies.

Stabilizing jacks are just that: They are for steadying, not leveling. No jack should be used for lev-

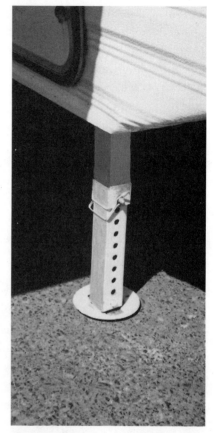

Figure 8-12. *The pin arrangement for securing a fifth-wheel trailer's front jacks.*

eling unless the instructions specify that it can be used for this purpose.

Fore-and-aft leveling of a conventional trailer is accomplished by raising or lowering the tongue jack. It's necessary to understand how the front jacks of a fifth-wheel trailer are designed to effectively use them for fore-and-aft leveling. The jack consists of three box-like sections, with two that telescope inside the fixed upper section. The up-and-down movement of the outer telescoping section, or ram tube, inside the fixed section is gear-controlled. The distance of travel from stop to stop can be from 12 to 16 inches. The pad tube, the inner section of the jack (the part in contact with the ground), is a leg that slides into and out of the ram tube; it slides out of the ram tube when the spring clip holding it in place is released. Before the clip is released, however, the ram tube usually must be lowered; how much depends on how level the campsite is from front to back. On some trailers the lowering is done with electricity—a 12-volt motor; on others it is done manually with a handle. The switch for electric jacks is located either under the gooseneck or on the street side just behind the gooseneck, where the socket for manual jacks is also located. The jack control may be in a locking compartment.

The ram tube should be lowered enough so that once the trailer is unhitched, there is sufficient length of travel to lower the trailer to where it is level. In most campsites, lowering the ram tube a few inches provides enough travel; it is the unusual site that would necessitate lowering the ram tube as far as it goes. The ability to judge this comes with practice. After the ram tube is lowered, release the pad tube and let it fall to the ground.

The pin that secures the pad tube fits through one set of the numerous paired holes along each side of the pad tube, and through a pair of holes in the lower end of the ram tube (Figure 8-12). If the holes in the two sections don't line up after one pad tube has been dropped and is resting on the ground, slightly raise or lower the ram tube until they do. When the other pad tube is dropped on uneven ground, its holes may not line up; a piece of ¼- or ½-inch plywood (or both) placed under the pad tube should raise it the necessary amount. Both jacks should always bear an equal amount of trailer weight for stability and to avoid premature jack failure.

When the pad tube is secured by the pin to the ram tube, raise the trailer enough so that the jacks support the trailer's weight (with electric jacks, the motor changes its sound as the jacks take the weight; with manual jacks, the handle becomes harder to turn). Make sure the pins are in place and the pad tubes are on the ground supporting the weight of the trailer; then the trailer can be unhitched. After the truck is pulled ahead enough to move it from under the gooseneck, the trailer is ready to be leveled.

In the unusual circumstance of a campsite that is considerably higher in the back than in the front, the ram tube may need no lowering because the front of the trailer needs to be raised to level it. In this case, release the pad tubes, secure them, and proceed as described previously.

The front jacks of a fifth-wheel trailer perform somewhat of a

Figure 8-13. *A stabilizing jack is often used on the kingpin box of a fifth-wheel trailer. (Courtesy BAL RV Products Group)*

stabilizing function—if the front of the trailer isn't elevated too much—but many trailerists also use a stabilizing jack at the far front end, at the kingpin box, for additional support (Figure 8-13). A stabilizing jack is not necessary; it's a matter of personal preference.

Using the Campground's Washroom

With several occupants in the RV, or if the RV bath is small or not private enough, it may be more convenient to use the campground's toilet and shower facilities. Some people use campground facilities because they don't want to clean their own bath or because they use their shower as a storage area. For whatever reason, if you use the washroom, it should be convenient to do so.

Some of our early RVs had no shower so we had no choice but to use campground washrooms. We developed a procedure that may work for you or give you some ideas to adapt.

We each had a bag containing our washroom necessities: soap, towel, personal grooming items, change of clothes, and quarters in case the showers were coin-operated (undressed and ready to bathe is no time to realize the shower is coin-operated). Each bag was large, made of sturdy canvas, with a flat, reinforced bottom, open top, and a handle on each side. Working out of the bag was easy because the stiff canvas prevented the sides from collapsing when it was set down. If there was no place to set the bag, it was hung by its handles on a hook. The bag was also handy when just the lavatory was used. We put all items back in the bag when we were finished with them so there was no chance of leaving something behind. The bags, being fabric, could be folded flat for convenient storage.

In addition to being spotlessly clean and having a plentiful supply of hot water, an ideal shower has an area outside the stall with a privacy door or curtain, a bench or stool, and a large hook or two on the wall. Many campground showers meet these criteria, but some do not.

Even a washroom that appears sparkling clean may not be hygienic. Unless disinfected regularly (after each use), a public shower is a place where you can pick up athlete's foot. Protect against this by always wearing thongs for showering and never stepping on a washroom floor with bare feet.

Don't assume supplies will be in a washroom; there may be paper towels but no soap. Toilet paper is usually supplied, but it's wise to keep a roll in your bag just in case. Toilet seat covers are not often provided.

Breaking Camp

Breaking camp involves undoing everything you did to set up. These duties can also be done in almost any order, as long as they are all done. It's most important that nothing involved with breaking camp be forgotten. When setting up, if you forget to connect the sewer hose, you can do so when you remember it, but if you forget to disconnect it before pulling out of the site, the hose or its fittings may be damaged.

If you don't have a checklist for anything else, have one for breaking camp. If you use the list every time you break camp, you won't be among the RVers we often see on the highway with the TV antenna up, entry steps down, roof vents and windows open, unsecured compartment doors flapping, or sewer cap dangling.

Some RVers evidently think that lowering the TV antenna is of primary importance. We have heard of RVers who go to the extreme of hanging the ignition keys on the antenna control handle inside the RV as a reminder to lower it, but they have no reminders for more important tasks, such as disconnecting the water and sewer hoses and the shore-power cable. With a checklist containing all major and minor tasks, you won't be likely to forget anything.

To be really useful, a checklist must be detailed and contain everything that applies to your particular rig. The hitching steps on a list for fifth-wheel and conventional trailers are different, and a motorhome list won't have any hitching steps (unless an auxiliary vehicle is towed; then include all the steps for attaching a tow bar or tow dolly).

Because a detailed list can be lengthy, it may be easier to use if it is divided into two sections. One section of our list applies to all tasks that need to be done inside the trailer; the other, to outside tasks. In addition to the common items that would be included on any RVer's list (close windows and roof vents; clear counters and tables; lower TV antenna; stow TV in a safe place; turn off lights, radio, and furnace; secure refrigerator and cabinet doors), our inside list reminds us to latch the sliding door on the bath, lock the slideout pantry in place, put the circuit analyzer in the galley receptacle, and turn off the refrigerator (we don't travel with it on). Another RVer's inside list may contain items such as set refrigerator mode for travel, retract slideout(s), turn over freestanding furniture, secure shower door, empty pet's water dish, and raise blinds (blinds rattle when a motorhome is moving and the noise may annoy occupants; in any moving RV, blinds should not swing free).

The first item on our outside list is: remove the kingpin stabilizing jack. A separate entry (because it's easy to forget) reminds us to stow the removable handle used with the jack. Other outside items include: raise rear stabilizing jacks, empty holding tanks, close valves, replace sewer pipe cap, store sewer hose, turn off water heater, lower and latch front and rear stone shields, stow TV cable, unplug shore-power cable, and store outside doormat in truck's bed.

All the steps involved in hitching are listed in the order in which they are done: remove safety pin from hitch handle and open hitch jaws, lower truck tailgate, remove TECC from the kingpin box, and raise (or lower) front of trailer. After all these steps are completed, the trailer is hitched (this is not on our list; we've never once forgotten it). The remaining hitch-related items are: check that hitch jaws are closed, shut tailgate, attach breakaway cable, insert safety pin in hitch handle, plug in TECC, raise front trailer jacks and secure them, and remove wheel chock. Although our hitching procedure is a set routine, the list provides a doublecheck and confirms that the entire procedure has been completed.

If you hook up to city water, include disconnecting and storing the water hose; if a water-pressure regulator is used, include this often forgotten item. Other items on an outside list may be: secure awning, and stow lawn chairs and barbecue grill.

Because we are extra cautious when breaking camp, in addition to faithfully using a checklist, we also do a "walkaround" of the trailer and tow vehicle after hitching. Many of the same items that have already been checked off the list are covered, but because we go inside to wash our hands after hitching and taking care of other outside chores, on the way to the door it takes no time at all to make a visual check of all the items listed above. Doing a walkaround is a good habit to form.

On the bottom of each list is a section with the final tasks. Inside: Put the soap container away and turn off the water pump switch. Outside: Lock the entry door, fold up door step, check lights (the one who isn't driving the first leg stands at the rear of the trailer and, as the turn signals, emergency flashers, truck and trailer brake lights, and running lights are activated, indicates by hand signals that all are working properly), remove leveling boards (after the trailer has been driven off), and lock the compartment after they have been put away.

We have yet another list, a short one we call "the lunch list." If we stop to prepare lunch in the trailer, the list reminds us to close all roof vents and windows, switch off the radio, turn off the propane cylinders, and switch off the water pump.

When traveling with children, it takes a little longer to break camp because toys and bicycles need to be collected from around the campsite and secured for travel (put these items on the checklist). If you have eaten meals at the picnic table or used it for other activities, check under and around the table for forgotten items. After the rig has been pulled out of the site, go back and look over the site carefully to be sure nothing has been left behind. If you've taken care of everything on your checklist, you're ready to depart; just don't go off and leave a load of laundry in the dryer and, more important, be sure all family members and pets are aboard!

One last thing: If you have a trailer with electric brakes, check that the brakes are working by using the manual override lever on the brake controller. Do this on the campground road, before entering the highway.

Depending on a checklist won't work if you have to remember where you put it each time you want to use it. Have a special place to store it where it's handy so there is no excuse for not using it every time you break camp.

The cockpit of a motorhome or tow vehicle is not the place to keep the list. When you climb into the cockpit, you are presumably ready to go; the list should be accessible for use while breaking camp. We keep our lists in a cabinet near the entry door. They are stored in a pocket (the bottom 3 inches of a 6 x 9 manila envelope, which is large enough to hold the lists and a pencil) attached to the inside of the cabinet door with double-faced mounting tape.

In describing checklist entries, we have used lengthy phrases, but you'll probably use your own shorthand on your lists. For example, instead of listing "lower TV antenna" and "turn off refrigerator," "TV antenna" and "refrigerator" should suffice.

Chapter 9

Safety for You and Your RV

The changes of society in general are often reflected in the smaller RVing society. These changes include ever-mounting increases in burglaries and vandalism. RVers should be aware that these crimes may affect them when they are RVing just as when they are at home.

Be Particular About Where You Park Your Rig

To avoid being a victim of crimes, be cautious about where you park your rig, be it for a few minutes in a parking lot, overnight in a highway rest area, or even in certain campgrounds. When we stop for shopping or a restaurant meal, we try to park our rig where it is highly visible because thieves and vandals prefer to work unobserved.

In states that allow it, overnighting in highway rest areas is a practice among some RVers; however, never assume that these places are safe. All types of people use these rest areas, some for the sole purpose of stealing from others. We do not recommend overnighting in a rest area if you don't have a toilet in your RV. Most problems arise when the occupants leave the RV to use the public toilet. Someone may attack you for the valuables you may be carrying, or they may enter the RV to steal whatever can be taken quickly and perhaps harm anyone remaining in the RV.

Be suspicious of anyone who knocks on your door in a rest area (or anywhere else) if you are not expecting anyone. Keep the door closed and locked, turn on the outside light, ask for identification, and find out what the person wants. If you have reason to doubt the person, don't open the door. Ask to have identification shown at a window and use a flashlight at night to inspect it. Law enforcement officers shouldn't

Figure 9-1. *Some campgrounds, such as the Pacific Shores Campground in Newport, Oregon, have a security check at the entrance.*

object to this. The information you receive must be the basis for your judgment about opening the door.

RVers are safe in most private campgrounds. The most secure campgrounds have an attendant on duty at the entrance who checks everyone entering and leaving (Figure 9-1), but not many campgrounds provide this level of security (those that do usually have higher than average rates). A campground that is well lit after dark and has a manager living on the premises is fairly secure. Other RVers in a campground provide an additional measure of security.

Security in public campgrounds can range from good to none at all. The safest have people on regular patrol night and day, and an entrance attendant who stops anyone without a valid receipt for a site. Even without stringent controls, you should have few concerns about safety if a host is present. Some county or city parks are patrolled periodically by local law enforcement officers whether or not there is a host.

We enjoy staying in public campgrounds because they are often in beautiful surroundings and are relatively uncrowded; nonetheless, we are especially watchful in such campgrounds. We keep an eye on those who cruise around or pull into a site without an RV or visible camping gear. If we must leave the campground when these noncampers are around, we unobtrusively jot down the license number and make and model of their vehicle. We are happy to report that in our many years of RVing, we have never had to use this information.

Crowded public campgrounds are favorite operating areas for

thieves. People are apt to leave valuables on picnic tables and around the campsite. It's easy for thieves to walk away with equipment that is left unattended for even a few minutes. It's best to keep valuables out of view: Thieves who can't see your camera, binoculars, camcorder, radio, or portable cassette player won't know you have items worth stealing. Equipment used outdoors (folding chairs, barbecue grills, coolers, and bicycles) should be taken inside the RV or secured outside when you are away from your campsite. Some RVers run a chain through this equipment and padlock it to an immovable object, such as the RV's bumper or axle. Because outside compartments may contain valuables or open to the interior of the RV, close and lock them when they aren't in use. Also keep roof storage pods and truckbed tool boxes locked. If you go to another part of the campground where you can't see the door to your RV, lock the door—even for just a few minutes—to prevent burglars from simply walking in.

Thieves can also enter through windows. It's easy to get through the opening on a large sliding window, but entry is difficult through any size louvered window. If you want to leave windows open when you are away, open only sliding windows that are too small for even a child to enter (some years ago we heard of a family of thieves who used their children to enter RVs through small windows and roof vents). Don't leave open any windows near entry doors; the screen can be pushed in, and someone could reach around and unlock the door from the inside. The same holds true for an escape window if it has an opening portion for ventilation. It may be possible for someone to reach in and release the safety latch (Figure 9-2).

Figure 9-2. *Don't leave the escape window open if you will be away from your RV. Someone with a long arm could reach around and unlatch the window. The square latch handle on this window is on the right side, behind the drapery tieback.*

Do not leave valuable items in a vehicle where they can be seen. Even if the vehicle is locked, expensive items are tempting targets for

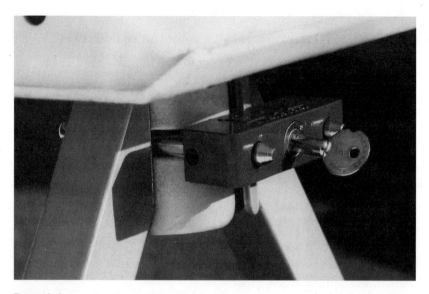

Figure 9-3. *It is harder for thieves to steal a trailer if a hitch lock is used. Shown here is a kingpin lock for a fifth-wheel trailer.* (Courtesy BAL RV Products Group)

thieves. Keep them out of sight in a console or under the seat at all times. Although loose equipment is stolen most often, an RV, auxiliary vehicle, or tow vehicle is sometimes the objective of thieves.

Because motorhomes can be driven away, they are stolen more often than trailers, which require a tow vehicle to move them. Nevertheless, when a fifth-wheel or conventional trailer or tow dolly is parked, it's wise to put a lock on the hitch. Locks are available for all types of hitches (Figure 9-3). When you park your vehicle, roll up the windows, lock the doors, and never leave keys in the ignition.

To further safeguard a vehicle, a device that locks the steering wheel can be used, or a system can be installed that causes the vehicle's engine to die about 30 seconds after it is started and prevents restarting.

When we are inside our trailer, we keep the door locked so no one can just walk in—an unlikely but possible occurrence. In warm weather, when the door is left open, the screen door is secured with a hook and eye. It was installed about 2 feet down from the top of the door so no one can push the slider back and reach in to undo the hook. Of course, with a little effort, the hook can still be reached through the slider opening, but its unusual location delays anyone intent on breaking in, giving us a little time to react. In addition to the regular door latch, which is not very sturdy and can be opened with a master key, every RV should have a deadbolt lock.

We don't want to give the impression that RVing is fraught with risks; it's not. We've been RVing for many years without ever having anything stolen, and we feel secure in most campgrounds. RVing wouldn't be much fun if we were constantly on guard and worrying about theft. The best ways to avoid these worries are:

- Use common sense when selecting a place to park your rig.

- For short stops, park your rig where it is highly visible.

- Be wary about opening the door to strangers.

- Lock the entry door when you leave the RV, even for just a few minutes, particularly if the door won't be in your view.

- Keep outside compartment doors locked.

- Leave open only small sliding windows when you are gone.

- Close any window next to a door or in an escape window.

- Don't leave unsecured or unattended valuables in view.

- Secure motorized vehicles before you leave them unoccupied.

- Lock the door when you are inside the RV.

- Make it difficult for thieves to get what they want; if they can't steal something easily, they may leave it alone.

Fire Prevention

Theft is an outside element that can threaten RVers, but there are other safety concerns to be aware of as well. A fire in an RV can be more devastating than the theft of valuables, yet some RVers who carefully secure their belongings have a casual attitude about fire prevention and equipping their units with fire extinguishers.

Prevention is mostly common sense: being careful with lighted cigarettes and candles, and keeping flammable items away from heat sources and open flames (electric heaters and range burners). When an RV comes from the manufacturer, a galley window near the range doesn't have a curtain, only a window shade or mini-blind. It's best to leave this window uncurtained; keep this in mind if you redecorate.

Don't overload electrical circuits. Any equipment powered by electricity or propane should be clean and in proper working order. Keep the furnace compartment and all visible elements of the furnace free from dust, and allow nothing to obstruct ducts and vents. Be sure the water heater is operating properly and the flame is adjusted to the right height. It is common to see RVs with black soot streaks emanating from the water-heater compartment—a sign that either the flame is too high or the burner chamber is defective; both are potential fire hazards.

RV manufacturers are required to install only one fire extinguisher; however, all except the smallest RVs should have two or more, one of which should be handy in the galley. Motorhomes and tow vehicles should have an extinguisher in the cockpit. All extinguishers should be easily accessible. Wall mounting is a good method of installation because the extinguisher can't get buried in a storage compartment. When purchasing a used RV, make sure it is equipped with an adequate number of fire extinguishers in working order.

RVs are factory-equipped with a 5BC-rated extinguisher. The numeral designates the amount of retardant in the extinguisher; the letters designate the type of fires the retardant will extinguish: A for flammable materials such as paper and wood, B for flammable liquids such as petroleum-based products and cooking oils, and C for electrical fires. The retardant in BC-rated extinguishers is sodium bicarbonate (baking soda). While not a substitute for a fire extinguisher, baking soda can be used to douse small fires; many RVers keep a box handy in the galley.

When a fire occurs, it is too late to learn how to use an extinguisher. Read the instructions several times until you are familiar with its operation. Don't test-fire any extinguisher that is intended to fight a fire. The only extinguisher that should ever be test-fired is one that is purchased solely as a practice unit, and it's a good idea to use one for practice so all occupants of the RV can learn how to use it. Everyone should also know where the escape windows are and how they operate. On many, the bottom of the window swings out after releasing spring-loaded handles in the bottom corners.

Periodically (and always before using the RV), check the extinguishers to make sure they are in proper working order. On some extinguishers is a gauge that indicates their condition. Others have a test button and instructions for making a condition test.

Most extinguishers for RVs are small and cannot be recharged. If the test button or gauge indicates a deficiency, replace the extinguisher (suitable extinguishers can be purchased for under $15). Sodium bicarbonate can settle and become compacted from vibration, so a BC-rated extinguisher should be rapped sharply on its side and bottom before use.

All new RVs are equipped with a smoke detector, and one should be installed in an older RV if not so equipped. Small detectors are available at RV supply stores. Check the smoke detector's battery whenever you make the periodic and pre-trip checks on your extinguishers.

If a fire occurs and is very small and contained, one person can remain to fight it; otherwise, all occupants should immediately exit the RV. If the fire is large and spreading rapidly, fire extinguishers will not put it out; get everyone out and call the fire department.

Shut off what is fueling the fire, if you can do so safely. In the case of a fire on the galley range, turn off all burners. If a fire is in the furnace, water heater, or refrigerator, shut off the entire propane supply at the cylinders. Unplug any electrical appliance that catches fire and also disconnect the shore-power cable from the campsite's hookup. If the RV is equipped with a battery switch (more common on motorhomes than trailers), turn it off to stop the current flow if a fire originates in a 12-volt system or appliance.

Safety Practices with a Propane System

RVers depend on propane for cooking, heating, hot water, and often for refrigeration. Propane is easy to use and the propane system on most RVs provides years of trouble-free service. It is because propane serves us so well and conveniently that many RVers take this potentially dangerous substance for granted and forget that it needs to be dealt with properly to avoid accidents.

If you smell the distinctive rotten-onion odor of propane when entering your RV, a dangerous situation exists. Propane, being heavier than air, settles to the lowest point in the RV. A concentration of propane will explode if the tiniest spark or flame reaches it, so exercise extreme caution to prevent this. Be careful of *any* metal-to-metal contact that could cause a spark, and do not use the water pump—in most RVs, the pump is located on the floor, where the propane settles.

Follow these steps if you smell propane when entering your RV:

• Do nothing to cause a spark or flame.

• Leave the door open.

• Turn off the main propane supply at the cylinders.

• Open all windows.

• Wait outside until the gas dissipates.

After these steps are completed, then and only then, check for leaks. Apply soapy water to valves, joints, and pipes where you suspect a leak; bubbles appear at the leak. NEVER TRY TO TRACE A PROPANE LEAK BY USING AN OPEN FLAME. Unless the leak can be fixed by tightening a loose connection, call a propane repairperson to take care of the problem. Devices that sound an alarm when gas is detected are available at RV supply stores.

When using unvented propane equipment, such as a catalytic heater, a window must be open so fresh air can enter to replenish the oxygen. Never use the galley range to heat the RV.

When we travel, our propane cylinders are always turned off. By following this practice, we are never concerned about an open flame when we stop for fuel. RVers who run their refrigerator on propane while traveling must be sure to turn it off before fueling. A water heater and, often forgotten, the pilot light on a range also must be turned off.

Follow safety practices when refilling propane cylinders. If a cylinder must be transported to be filled, carry it in the position in which it is mounted on the RV; do not turn upright cylinders on their side and vice versa. Some state laws require that a plug be in the valve when a cylinder is transported.

Trailer cylinders are removable and thus can be filled by weight or volume; motorhome cylinders, which are not removable, are filled by volume only. All cylinders are equipped with a safety feature called an 80-percent valve. Before the refilling supply hose is attached to a removable cylinder, the operator should loosen the 80-percent valve with a screwdriver; the safety valve on most motorhomes is a plug that can be loosened with the fingers. Overfilling is prevented because propane escapes from the valve when the cylinder is filled to 80-percent of capacity; 20 percent is left for expansion. (Some motorhomes are equipped with an automatic stop-fill valve.) When propane issues from the safety valve, the supply should be shut off immediately.

Filling is sometimes done by a gallon meter. Never allow the operator to fill by just reading the gallon meter; insist that the 80-percent valve be open. And don't let operators do you "a favor" by giving you an extra gallon over your cylinder's capacity (this is stamped on the cylinder). The regulator can be damaged by overfilling. In hot weather, when fuel expands, the relief valve will open, spilling the excess propane, which settles to the ground. Overfilling may even cause the cylinder to rupture. A rupture nearly always results in an explosion. When we have an overfilled cylinder—sometimes the operator doesn't turn off the valve quickly enough—the 80-percent valve is opened to vent the excess.

Operators who fill cylinders are supposed to be trained to do the job properly, but many are not. A bulk propane supply outlet is about the only place where you can be assured that the operator is properly trained. Untrained operators at other propane filling stations too often have a cavalier attitude about the dangerous substance they are handling. We've encountered many operators who were unaware of the 80-percent valve. Once we had a cylinder filled at a farm supply store— the only place nearby where propane was available. The operator neglected to turn off the supply before he disconnected the hose; fortunately, nothing serious happened when the writhing, high-pressure hose spewed fuel in all directions.

When a cylinder is 12 years old, it must be recertified by an authorized propane dealer. Bulk suppliers have personnel trained to do the recertification.

Carbon Monoxide

Carbon monoxide (CO) is a highly poisonous gas that must not be allowed to enter an RV. Often the occupants don't know it is present because it is odorless and colorless. A slight headache, which is often not attributed to CO, is the first symptom of the poisoning.

CO is a by-product of an internal combustion engine. It can enter the living quarters of a motorhome if the propulsion engine's exhaust system is faulty—a rare occurrence. Motorhomers should be more concerned with the CO from a built-in generator. It's not so rare to hear about motorhomers who died because they were careless about the operation of a built-in generator.

The smallest leak in the generator's exhaust system can allow gas to seep into the living area. Even if the exhaust system is sound, CO can enter an open window or door near the generator compartment, or be blown in by the wind. *It is extremely dangerous to run a generator when occupants of the RV are sleeping.*

Any motorhome built after September 1, 1993, has a CO-detector installed; an alarm sounds if gas is present. A detector should be added on an older motorhome; installation is easy. Battery-operated models or the type that is installed in the 12-volt system are available in RV supply stores. A combination CO/propane detector is also available. Ensuring that the CO detector is operative should be on your checklist.

As with second-hand smoke from cigarettes, second-hand CO emissions are dangerous. If your RV is parked where it receives fumes from the generator in another RV, you and other occupants of your RV are in danger. Wind can blow fumes your way, which is particularly dangerous if your RV is parked close to buildings or shrubbery or in between other RVs, where air can't circulate freely.

Always be alert for conditions that could cause CO from your generator or an outside source to enter your RV.

Chapter 10

Cleaning and Maintenance

Cleaning the interior of an RV is not much different than house-cleaning, and, in most respects, cleaning the exterior is much like washing an automobile. Products and equipment specifically designed for RV applications are available at RV supply stores.

Cleaning the Interior

The only difference between cleaning floor coverings in your residence and those in your RV is that a small vacuum, broom, or carpet sweeper is more suitable than a larger household model.

To help keep floors and carpeting clean, place a mat or small rug just inside the entry door and another at the bottom of the outside steps, and cover each step with a rug (securely anchored so they won't come off during travel). Take care to avoid tracking in sand; the abrasiveness wears out carpeting and scratches vinyl floor coverings.

Most likely your RV upholstery, window coverings, cabinets, and countertops can be cleaned with the same methods and products used at home, but check the owner's manual for any special instructions.

Defrosting the Refrigerator

RV refrigerators are not self-defrosting. Perhaps in the future the technology for making a self-defrosting absorption-type refrigerator will be developed, but until then, RV refrigerators have to be defrosted the old-fashioned way when ice collects on the cooling fins or in the freezer.

Consult the refrigerator instruction manual for defrosting methods. Usually, the recommended procedure is to shut off the unit, remove the food, and place pans of hot water on the shelves to melt the ice. Do not direct a hair dryer at the fins—the heat may warp them. Meltwater from

Figure 10-1. *The cooling fins and drip tray of an RV refrigerator.*

the cooling fins runs into the drip tray (Figure 10-1). Too much meltwater will fill the water container on the back of the refrigerator (evaporation takes care of the normal amount of water that collects in the container). To keep the container from overflowing, use a sponge to remove excess water (the container is accessed from the outside refrigerator compartment). The meltwater in a separate freezer compartment has to be sponged up because there is no drain in the freezer.

We often defrost the refrigerator section simply by turning the refrigerator off before we go to bed and turning it back on in the morning. If we haven't waited too long to defrost, ice buildup on the fins is gone by morning. Stored foods remain safely cold because the refrigerator's interior temperature rises only two or three degrees while it's turned off.

Unless you use your RV continuously for several weeks, ice does not build up enough to warrant defrosting during a trip.

Cleaning the Bath and Black-Water Holding Tank
RV toilets shouldn't be cleaned with the harsh chemicals used for residential toilets. Don't use chlorine bleach or any products containing bleach because it destroys rubber seals and gaskets. If the toilet is made

of plastic (as many RV toilets are), don't use an abrasive cleanser on it, or on a tub, shower enclosure, or lavatory made of plastic or fiberglass. Wiping a surface with full-strength vinegar removes lime deposits.

The gray-water holding tank doesn't need to be cleaned because there are no solids or toilet paper in it, but each time the black-water tank is emptied, open the toilet trap for a few seconds to let some water flush out the tank. More thorough cleaning can be done with a special tool designed for this purpose: a long wand that attaches to a hose. The wand reaches into the holding tank through the toilet trap. When it's in place, it can be manipulated so the water spray reaches all corners of the tank.

For easier holding-tank cleaning, many RVers use biodegradable toilet tissue, which dissolves rather than clumps, as ordinary toilet tissue does. Never put anything other than toilet paper in the toilet.

Numerous products are available to eliminate holding-tank odors.

Outside Maintenance

Many cleaning products are available for an RV's exterior, whether it is fiberglass or painted or unpainted aluminum: washes, waxes, black-streak removers, shine and gloss restorers, and protectants, along with hose attachments such as wands and brushes (Figure 10-2).

RVs need to be washed periodically to remove road dust and grime, but whether you want to wax your unit is a matter of personal preference. A trailer we had for seven years was never waxed, yet when we sold it, its finish looked as shiny as the day it left the dealer's lot.

A little elbow grease and perhaps a suitable product are needed

Figure 10-2. *Washing the upper portions of an RV is easy if you have a long-handled brush.* (Courtesy Adjust-A-Brush)

to remove black streaks, which appear most often on the sides of the RV under windows and where the sides join the roof. Dirt collects under window and joint trim, and rain causes it to run out as black streaks.

As a rubber roof ages, a fine powder develops on the surface. If the roof is hosed down, the powder causes chalky white streaks on the RV's sides. If the roof is scrubbed with a brush, more powder is removed and more residue appears on the sides. Therefore, when cleaning a unit with a rubber roof, do the roof first. After washing a roof section, rinse the side under it as soon as possible to remove any powder residue. Your owner's manual may outline cleaning methods and contain specific product recommendations.

Sanitizing the Potable-Water Tank

The water tank in a new RV should be sanitized before use, and this should also be done to the tank on a used RV and a unit that has been stored for a long period. An RV stored for the winter shouldn't require tank sanitizing in the spring, however.

To completely disinfect the tank, prepare a solution of 1 gallon of water to ¼ cup of chlorine bleach. With the tank empty, use the fill spout to pour in 1 gallon of solution for each 15 gallons of capacity. Fill the tank with water. Open all faucets, both hot and cold, and let the water run until a distinct chlorine odor is detected. Shut the faucets. Let the water remain in the tank and system for 3 hours. (If the solution is ½ cup of bleach to 1 gallon of water, the standing time is reduced to 1 hour.) Using the faucets and the tank drain, flush and drain the system. Fill the tank with fresh water.

If a chlorine taste remains in the water, prepare a solution of 1 quart of vinegar to 5 gallons of water, or ½ cup of baking soda to 1 gallon of water. Pour the solution into the tank and fill it with water. Either let the mixture sit overnight or hasten the purifying process by driving the rig to agitate the mixture. After flushing and draining again, fill the tank with fresh water.

Battery Maintenance

Unless a battery is a no-maintenance, or sealed, type, it needs maintenance to prolong its life. Water must be added periodically to the fluid, or electrolyte; use only distilled water for this purpose. We use a small paper cup creased to form a spout for pouring the water; this directs the water into the tiny cell opening.

For the best service, battery posts should be free of corrosion. A baking-soda solution dissolves corrosion. It's handy to use a creased paper cup for this, too. Put a teaspoon of baking soda in a 3½-ounce paper cup and fill it with water. Pour some of the solution on the post; after a few seconds, the corrosion dissolves. Wipe up any residue with a dry paper towel; then, with a damp paper towel, thoroughly wipe the treated area. Make sure the battery caps are on before cleaning the posts to prevent the baking-soda solution from entering the cells.

You must be extremely careful when working with a battery; improper handling can result in fire and personal injuries, including burns and blindness from contact with sulfuric-acid electrolyte. Do not smoke around a battery; a battery produces hydrogen gas, which is an explosive. Always wear old clothes, rubber gloves, and goggles or safety glasses when working on a battery. Be sure a supply of baking soda (which neutralizes sulfuric acid) and fresh water is close by; if a faucet isn't handy, keep a bucket of water next to you.

If sulfuric acid gets into your eyes despite your having taken these precautions, flush your eyes repeatedly with several changes of fresh water and immediately see an ophthalmologist. For burns caused by sulfuric acid on the skin, sprinkle baking soda on the affected area, then flush well with water.

If you live in a cold climate, the battery should be removed from the RV for winter storage (more about this later). When using wrenches to remove battery cables from the posts, avoid touching both posts at the same time; this causes arcing and sparking, which can result in burns. It's best to remove any rings before working on a battery—if a metal ring shorts out between a battery post and a wrench, it can become red hot and melt.

Where batteries are concerned, never become lax about safety precautions and don't be careless.

General Maintenance

Periodically check all safety pins, safety chains, and any other equipment where metal rubs against metal for signs of wear, cracks, or rust;

replace or repair what is needed. Also check every visible screw or bolt on the RV and on hitches for tightness—don't overlook the bolts used to attach the hitch to the tow vehicle, those in a trailer's suspension system, and the screws on roof ladders.

Check for cracks in caulking and recaulk if necessary; don't forget the caulking around items mounted on the roof. Inspect weather stripping on entry doors and outside storage compartments to see if it has pulled away or become badly flattened; replace it if necessary.

If your RV has an enclosed underbody, be sure it is intact and the fastening devices are secure. Tears in some flexible underbody material can be patched with tape.

Lubricate any equipment where motion of metal against metal occurs, such as hitch balls and spring-bar sockets, with the one exception of the sway-control bar—never use lubricant on the slide bar.

The automotive components of motorhomes and tow vehicles should be serviced according to manufacturers' specifications. On trailers, the brakes should be checked and wheel bearings repacked once a year or every 10,000 miles. Lubricate tow-dolly bearings on the same schedule.

Pests

If there is a way to get in, pests will find it, whether the RV is being used or stored. A common problem is mice—they can enter through any openings in the bottom of the RV, such as around plumbing pipes. In addition to making a mess, mice can gnaw through electric wires and hoses on generators and motorhome engines.

Mice can be kept out by filling any bottom openings with steel or bronze wool. Bronze wool is more expensive, but it won't rust; it's available at marine supply stores. If the wool won't stay in, use clear mailing tape, which is sticky and water-resistant, to hold it in place. Mice may also come up the shore-power cable. If you store your RV during the winter with the shore-power cable plugged in, you may want to make a mouse guard to keep mice out. It's a circular piece of thin metal about 6 or 7 inches in diameter, with a hole in the center just big enough to fit snugly over the cable, and a slit from the edge to the hole for placing it on the cable. When in place, the mouse guard is perpendicular to the cable, and tall and slippery enough so that mice can't climb over or around it. Alternatively, the hole where the shore-power cable exits can be stuffed with steel or bronze wool.

On motorhomes, a possible mouse entry is in the automotive heating and air conditioning system. During storage, all levers on the dashboard control should be in the "off" position; this closes all outside access. As a mouse preventive, some RVers swear by the method of placing mothballs in drawers and corners; evidently, the smell keeps mice away.

Ants can get inside an RV via the shore-power cable. Periodically spraying the cable with insecticide makes it an unappealing pathway.

In the spring, watch for birds scouting out your RV for nesting places. They may want to make their home in a refrigerator vent, a king-pin box (if it is open on the backside), or a range vent (if it is not covered with a grille).

Furnace ports are favorite nesting places for hornets and wasps. Spiders are attracted to the odor of propane and may set up housekeeping around the regulator.

Storing an RV Between Trips

Between trips, you should take the following steps to keep pests out, protect the RV from the elements, and make getting ready for the next trip easier.

- Empty the holding tanks before storing the RV at home or in a storage facility.

- Remove all perishable food from cabinets.

- Turn off the refrigerator. To prevent discharging the battery, be sure all refrigerator circuits, including that of the interior light, are off. (Consult your owner's manual for storage procedures.)

- Remove all food from the refrigerator and leave the door open. Place a box of baking soda or a few charcoal briquettes in the refrigerator to remove odors.

- Clean the interior of the RV.

- If rain can't enter, slightly open one or two windows (if the RV is stored in a secure place where it's not likely to be broken into).

- Pull shades or close blinds.

- Turn off propane cylinders and cover the regulator.

- Remove dust and road grime to protect the RV's finish from pitting and staining.

- If the awning is damp, unroll it and let it dry thoroughly before storing it rolled up. (If it needs cleaning, follow the manufacturer's recommendations.)

- Cover tires if they will be exposed to the sun. Ready-made snap-on covers or a piece of plywood can be used.

Some RVs have 12-volt equipment with a phantom load—a small but constant electrical load that is present in refrigerator control circuits, equipment with LED indicator lights or a memory (such as a stereo), and gas detectors (if wired into the 12-volt system). Although phantom loads are small, they can discharge a battery over time. If your RV has any equipment with a phantom load, shut off all circuits at the panel by removing all fuses or turning off all circuit breakers.

Winterizing an RV for Storage

How you winterize your RV depends on your region's climate and how often, if at all, you use the RV during the winter. Many of the following storage practices will not be necessary if the RV is used frequently or stored in a warm climate.

Do everything discussed previously for storing the RV between trips and, in addition, remove food, toiletries, and cleaning supplies with containers that would burst if frozen. Remove the battery.

If you clean the exterior of your RV before storing it, you won't have to do this chore in the spring. More importantly, it is easier to rid the RV of road grime, bugs, tree sap, bird droppings, and the multitude of other compounds that have been picked up if they are not allowed to stay on for several months. Cleaning preserves the RV's finish and prevents pitting and permanent staining.

The main concern in below-freezing temperatures is to protect the plumbing from freezing. On your final trip before a winter lay-up, empty the holding tanks at the last campground at which you stay or at a dump station. At home, empty the potable-water and water-heater tanks by using their drains. Check the water-heater instruction manual for the drain location. The potable-water tank drain is a petcock either on the side of or under the RV. Remove water from the toilet and plumbing by flushing with the water pump off. Empty the hot and cold water lines by opening faucets and using the water-line drains inside the RV on the floor (usually in a storage area near the water pump); the water runs out of a hose under the RV.

When the system is thoroughly drained, close all valves and fill the system with a non-toxic antifreeze (instructions are on the container). At least 2 gallons of antifreeze is needed. *IMPORTANT! Use only special water-line antifreeze for this purpose. Never use automotive antifreeze because it is a deadly poison.* If you don't want to freeze-proof the plumbing yourself, your RV service center can do it.

Seal all openings where rodents can enter and insects can nest: holding-tank vent pipes, outside refrigerator compartment and roof vent, power cord compartment, outside furnace ports, range-hood vent, and outside locker doors with vents. Never seal the vents on a battery compartment unless the battery has been removed.

If the RV is sheltered from rain and snow, crack open a screened window or roof vent at the front and rear for ventilation to keep it from smelling musty.

The heat from a couple of 120-volt AC, low-wattage lightbulbs burning inside will help dry out the air in an RV that is stored in a damp climate. Alternatively, a dehumidifier can be used.

To protect the RV from the weight of heavy snow or tree limbs that may blow down in strong winter winds, store it in a garage or under a structure with a sturdy roof. If this can't be done, the only other choice for protection from the elements—but not windfalls—is to cover the RV with a tarpaulin or a special cover that encloses the entire RV (tarpaulins cover only the roof unless the RV is very small). Most covers are made of a material that breathes, which is important in a damp climate because air circulation is vital to prevent mildew and condensation. If the RV isn't covered, at least cover the air conditioner.

Tires should be protected from the sun; damaging ultraviolet rays exist in the winter just as in the summer. Tires last longer if the RV's weight is taken off them. The RV can be safely propped up with properly placed concrete blocks or jack stands; never use stabilizing jacks for this purpose.

The RV battery should be fully charged, removed, and kept in a cool place where it cannot freeze. The battery will discharge if stored on a concrete floor; instead, set it on wood blocks. During storage, charge the battery a couple of times during the season with a trickle charge of 1 amp or more for about 12 hours. The battery can be left in the RV in a climate not subject to freezing temperatures. In this case, disconnect the cables to prevent corrosion and wrap the cable ends with plastic electrician's tape.

In a severely cold climate, a motorhome engine needs to be prepared for storage. Ask you dealer for advice if you are going to decommission the engine. If you intend to store it in operating order, change the oil and oil filter so dirty oil won't remain in the engine for months. While you are at it, replace the air filter so you don't have to do this job in the spring. Fill the fuel tank as full as possible so there is no space for condensation to form. Check the antifreeze level and add some if needed. The owner's manual lists other winterizing procedures, and may recommend that once a month the engine be run for half an hour or more, or driven at highway speed for 10 miles.

When it comes to winterizing, do not overlook the RV's generator engine, which also needs preparation before storage. Consult the owner's manual for proper procedures; the generator may need to be run periodically, too.

Check your owner's manual for the fine points of winterizing your particular RV. In the absence of a manual, your RV dealer can provide you with the necessary information, as well as supplies.

Spring Commissioning

If you have thoroughly cleaned the interior and exterior of your RV before storing it for the winter, little needs to be done in the spring. Reinstall the battery if it was removed, remove tape from sealed openings, flush antifreeze from the water lines (save the antifreeze container for instructions), commission a motorhome or generator engine (if necessary), and, other than performing the usual trip-readying tasks, you're ready to go.

Chapter 11

The Pleasures of RVing

Perhaps the two most attractive aspects of RVing are that it enables travelers to enjoy the outdoors and that it is an activity in which the whole family can participate. Children and adults can benefit from the education that traveling provides, the camaraderie of RVing clubs is open to you, and you can even do your part as a conservationist within the RVing lifestyle.

Clubs for RVers

RVers are friendly folks, so it's only natural that they get together and form clubs. In addition to the travel clubs mentioned in Chapter 5, all sorts of RVing clubs exist: Some are designed to appeal to all RVers, and some are oriented toward RVers with a common special interest other than RVing.

The Good Sam Club (annual dues, $19) offers numerous services and benefits, including a 10-percent discount at certain campgrounds, the opportunity to attend annual national and state Samborees, and enrolling in the Good Sam Emergency Road Service (2575 Vista Del Mar Drive, Ventura, California 93001; 1-800-234-3450).

As the name implies, Family Campers and RVers is a family-oriented group open to anyone interested in camping and RVing. Activities include national, regional, and retiree rallies. Dues are $38 for two years (4804 Transit Road, Building 2, Depew, New York 14043-4906; 716-668-6242 or 1-800-245-9755).

The Family Motor Coach Association, with dues of $35 for the first year, $25 annually thereafter, is another family-oriented club, but open to motorhome owners only (8291 Clough Pike, Cincinnati, Ohio 45244; 513-474-3622 or 1-800-543-3622).

Escapees, or SKPs, started as a club for fulltimers, but membership is now open to all RVers (Route 5, Box 310, Livingston, Texas 77351; 409-327-8873). This club is unique in that it operates several non-profit, co-op campgrounds where members can rent a full-hookup site at rates much lower than at typical private campgrounds. All the co-op campgrounds, and some other locations, have free, non-hookup areas where members can leave their RVs between trips. SKPs annual dues are $40.

Among the many special-interest clubs are the Handicapped Travel Club (see Chapter 1) and Loners on Wheels (LoW) (P.O. Box 1355, Poplar Bluff, Missouri 63902; 817-626-4538), which provides support to those who travel alone. LoW is not a mate-finding club—only single RVers can join; membership ends when a member begins RVing with a partner.

Owners of certain brands of RVs have the opportunity to join a club just for those who own the same brand. After you purchase such an RV, you will receive information on joining; if you purchase a used unit, you can write to the manufacturer to find out if a club exists for that brand.

The prime focus for most RVing clubs is fellowship, companionship, and sharing experiences with like-minded individuals. Nearly every club has an annual rally, where members can socialize with old friends and make new ones. State and local club chapters may have several rallies during the year, which are generally informal and loosely structured. A potluck dinner may culminate a weekend get-together of a few members in a nearby campground. National rallies can involve thousands of RVers. In the towns where these large rallies are held, the RVs are usually lined up row after row in a special area that has been converted to a temporary campground. RVing seminars and workshops are often held at these giant rallies, and evening activities may include well-known entertainers.

Most clubs provide a monthly, bi-monthly, or quarterly magazine or newsletter to members. Many clubs have chapters and divisions based on common interests other than RVing.

RVers as Conservationists

Many of us, RVers or not, are concerned that we may be using up some of our natural resources. Conservation is one way individuals can do their part to protect these resources. Sometimes the conservation is voluntary, sometimes mandatory, but anyone using an RV can't help becoming a conservationist in varying degrees. RVs are smaller than fixed dwellings, so, when living in an RV for a weekend, a vacation, or fulltime, fewer consumables are used.

Consider water: When camping without a water hookup, the RV's internal tank supplies the water. In this circumstance, most RVers try to conserve so the supply will last as long as possible. With the two of us, when we are consciously trying to conserve, the water in our 60-gallon tank can last five days or more, even with several showers (skimpy ones, to be sure). Ever since we became fulltimers, our normal practice when washing or showering is to turn off the water between soaping and rinsing, and adjust the flow of the shower head to provide just enough water to do the job.

The amount of water needed to flush an RV toilet may be measured in quarts on the high side and pints on the low side, whereas gallons are needed to flush even water-saving residential toilets. Of course, if RVers use a campground's toilet and shower facilities, the comparison isn't valid. In fact, some people showering away from home may use more water than normal because they aren't paying the utility bills.

Few RVs have dishwashers, so dishes are done the old-fashioned way, which doesn't require gallons of water. Most RVs aren't equipped with washers and dryers (a washer/dryer combination is an option on some large RVs), so, without having a washer close at hand, RVers can't conveniently toss a few items into the machine, and they tend to put off doing the laundry until there is a full load.

The exact figure can't be calculated, but, undoubtedly, the fewer gallons of water used by millions of RVers amounts to significant conservation.

Water is also conserved when showering because the size of an RV's hot-water tank is either 6 or 10 gallons; these few gallons don't go far unless water for showers is used conservatively. It doesn't take much propane (or electricity) to heat such a small amount of water; in the summer, you may find the pilot light is sufficient to heat the water to the desired temperature.

Because RVs are smaller than fixed dwellings, and because no campgrounds provide any more than 50 amps of power (30 is more common), it is impossible for RVers to consume the amount of electricity

Figure 11-1. *Many RVs have heated holding tanks and water lines, making them suitable for use in all seasons. (Courtesy Winnebago Industries, Inc.)*

used in a house or apartment; less energy is also used for heating (whether the heat comes from electricity or gas) and air conditioning.

Cleaning supplies, some of which may be toxic, are used in smaller quantities because the space to be cleaned is smaller and fewer items need to be cleaned in an RV.

Getting the Most from Your RV

Most RVing is done in the summer, but don't let that stop you from using your RV in the spring and fall—and, if your unit is suitable, in the winter as well (Figure 11-1). It's better for the RV and its equipment if it is used often, and it may be good for you and your family to refresh yourselves by getting away more frequently.

If your RV is kept at your residence, it can double as a well-appointed, private guest room when friends and family visit.

Another way to get the most from your RV is to keep it stocked with the things you need for quick, spontaneous getaways. What if you decide on a Saturday morning that you can't face another week-end of yardwork? Is your RV ready to go when you are, or do you need several days to prepare for even a weekend trip?

Unless you intend to eat in restaurants, stock your RV with a variety of food that doesn't need refrigeration and has a relatively long shelf life. Dry cereal, peanut butter, jelly, crackers, and a broad selection of canned food—meats, vegetables, fruits, juices, soups, and desserts—are good choices. Packaged entrees that need no refrigeration may also be included. Put enough dry milk to make pints or quarts in self-sealing plastic bags; store the bags in the container you will use to mix the milk. Keep on hand a supply of instant coffee and tea. Store sugar in a plastic container and use dry coffee creamer. Snacks are especially important when children are along; carry canned nuts, individually wrapped hard candy, and raisins and other dried fruits.

While some of this food is not the healthiest—most prepared and canned food is high in sodium and fat content—it can certainly be eaten occasionally.

Select food in packages that are impervious to humidity or drying out, or repackage the food in airtight containers. Don't choose food that is affected adversely by freezing or extreme heat. Be sure all packages and storage containers are insect- and vermin-proof. We have accumulated many various-sized plastic containers with airtight lids—all selected because they make the best use of each cabinet's storage space. We transfer nearly all types of food except canned goods from the original containers to plastic containers.

If a weekend of eating only canned and packaged food doesn't appeal to you, make a permanent list (yes, another list) of items to take from home. Include food that augments what is already stored in the RV. The list may include, among other foods, fresh bread, meat, and baked goods for desserts. If you have space in your home freezer, a special "getaway" section could be set aside for these items.

There won't be enough time to cool the RV's refrigerator if you want a quick getaway, so have a portable cooler for food that needs to be kept cold. So you won't have to stop for ice, put ice cubes from your home freezer into plastic bags and add them to the cooler. For longer-lasting ice, freeze water-filled 1- or 2-quart milk or juice cartons.

Equip the RV with dishes and flatware—disposable or non-disposable—as well as cooking utensils and cutlery. Don't forget to include a can opener, salt and pepper, and condiments that need no refrigeration.

Store in the RV sleeping bags or other bedding, towels, washcloths, soap, paper towels, and toilet paper. Permanently keep aboard toothbrushes, toothpaste, sun screen, shaving lotion, razors, makeup, combs, and other grooming items. If it's not practical to store aboard such items as an electric shaver and hair dryer, put them on the permanent list of things to take from home. Ideally, even clothing, from underwear to outerwear, should be kept in the RV.

For entertainment and amusement, keep a deck of cards, games, paperback books, and perhaps a small TV on board. If you regularly go on fishing or hiking trips in your RV, store the gear in the RV instead of unloading it after each trip.

Keep the water tank filled, but if you don't use the RV often enough that the water is replenished frequently, drain the tank periodically and refill it with fresh water.

With a well-stocked RV, you can leave quickly when the urge to get away overtakes you. Nothing will be forgotten, and you won't have to shop or search for necessary items to take from home.

○ ○ ○ ○ ○

Learning about an RV's systems and campground procedures may seem formidable, but acquiring this knowledge is easy. It won't be long before you can count yourself among the 28 million veteran RVers who have found how easy it is to participate in the RVing lifestyle.

We were duty-bound to point out the pitfalls and problems of purchasing and using an RV, but rest assured that you may never encounter most of them.

Using the information in this book should enable you to enjoy relatively trouble-free RVing and to experience all the joys the lifestyle affords—just one of which is exploring our beautiful country. Who knows? Perhaps you'll like RVing so much that when the time is right, you'll adopt it as your permanent lifestyle and become fulltimers, as we did.

 *Appendix*

State Tourism Offices

Alabama Bureau of Tourism and Travel
P.O. Box 4309
Montgomery, AL 36103-4309
Tel.: (205) 242-4169
Toll Free: 1-800-ALABAMA

Alaska Division of Tourism
P.O. Box 110801
TIA
Juneau, AK 99811-0801
Tel.: (907) 465-2010

Arizona Office of Tourism
1100 West Washington
Phoenix, AZ 85007
Tel.: (602) 542-8687

Arkansas Department of Parks and Tourism
One Capitol Mall
Dept. 7701
Little Rock, AR 72201
Tel.: (501) 682-7777
Toll Free: 1-800-NATURAL

California Division of Tourism
P.O. Box 1499
Dept. TIA
Sacramento, CA 95812-1499
Tel.: (916) 322-2881
Toll Free: 1-800-TO-CALIF

Colorado Tourism Board
P.O. Box 38700
Denver, CO 80238
Tel.: (303) 592-5410
Toll Free: 1-800-COLORADO
(1-800-265-6723)

Connecticut Department of Economic Development, Tourism Division
865 Brook St.
Rocky Hill, CT 06067
Tel.: (203) 258-4355
Toll Free: 1-800-CT-BOUND

Delaware Tourism Office
99 Kings Highway
Box 1401
Dept. TIA
Dover, DE 19903
Tel.: (302) 739-4271
Toll Free: 1-800-441-8846

Florida Division of Tourism
126 West Van Buren St.
FLDA
Tallahassee, FL 32399-2000
Tel.: (904) 487-1462

Georgia Department of Industry, Trade, & Tourism
P.O. Box 1776
Dept. TIA
Atlanta, GA 30301
Tel.: (404) 656-3590
Toll Free: 1-800-VISIT-GA

Hawaii Department of Business,
Economic Development, &
Tourism
P.O. Box 2359
Honolulu, HI 96804
Tel.: (808) 586-2423

Idaho Division of Tourism
Development
700 W. State St.
Dept. C
Boise, ID 83720
Tel.: (208) 334-2470
Toll Free: 1-800-635-7820

Illinois Bureau of Tourism
100 W. Randolph, Suite 3-400
Chicago, IL 60601
Tel.: (312) 814-4732
Toll Free: 1-800-223-0121

Indiana Department of
Commerce/Tourism and Film
Development Division
One North Capitol, Suite 700
Indianapolis, IN 46204-2288
Tel.: (317) 232-8860
Toll Free: 1-800-289-6646

Iowa Division of Tourism
200 East Grand
Des Moines, IA 50309
Tel.: (515) 242-4705
Toll Free: 1-800-345-IOWA (Ordering
vacation kit only) (U.S. only)
1-800-528-5265 (Special Events
Calendar)

Kansas Travel & Tourism Division
700 SW Harrison St., Suite 1300
Topeka, KS 66603-3712
Tel.: (913) 296-2009
Toll Free: 1-800-2KANSAS

Kentucky Department of Travel
Development
500 Mero St., 22nd Floor
Dept. DA

Frankfort, KY 40601
Tel.: (502) 564-4930
Toll Free: 1-800-225-TRIP

Louisiana Office of Tourism
Attn.: Inquiry Department
P.O. Box 94291
LOT
Baton Rouge, LA 70804-9291
Tel.: (504) 342-8119
Toll Free: 1-800-33-GUMBO

Maine Office of Tourism
189 State St.
Augusta, ME 04333
Tel.: (207) 289-5711
Toll Free: 1-800-533-9595

Maryland Office of Tourism
Development
217 East Redwood St., 9th Floor
Baltimore, MD 21202
Tel.: (410) 333-6611
Toll Free: 1-800-543-1036
(For vacation kit only)

Massachusetts Office of Travel and
Tourism
100 Cambridge St., 13th Floor
Boston, MA 02202
Tel.: (617) 727-3201
Toll Free: 1-800-447-MASS
(For vacation kit only) (U.S. only)

Michigan Travel Bureau
P.O. Box 3393
Livonia, MI 48151-3393
Tel.: (517) 373-0670
Toll Free: 1-800-5432-YES

Minnesota Office of Tourism
121 7th Place East
St. Paul, MN 55101
Tel.: (612) 296-5029
Toll Free: 1-800-657-3700

Mississippi Division of Tourism
P.O. Box 1705

Ocean Springs, MS 39566-1705
Tel.: (601) 359-3297
Toll Free: 1-800-WARMEST

Missouri Division of Tourism
P.O. Box 1055
Dept. TIA
Jefferson City, MO 65102
Tel.: (314) 751-4133
Toll Free: 1-800-877-1234

Travel Montana
Room TIA
Deer Lodge, MT 59722
Tel.: (406) 444-2654
Toll Free: 1-800-VISIT-MT

**Nebraska Division of Travel and
Tourism**
P.O. Box 94666
Lincoln, NE 68509
Tel.: (402) 471-3796
Toll Free: 1-800-228-4307

Nevada Commission on Tourism
Capitol Complex
Dept. TIA
Carson City, NV 89710
Tel.: (702) 687-4322
Toll Free: 1-800-NEVADA-8

**New Hampshire Office of Travel and
Tourism Development**
P.O. Box 856
Dept. TIA
Concord, NH 03302
Tel.: (603) 271-2343

**New Jersey Division of Travel and
Tourism**
20 West State St.
CN 826, Dept. TIA
Trenton, NJ 08625
Tel.: (609) 292-2470
Toll Free: 1-800-JERSEY-7

New Mexico Department of Tourism
491 Old Santa Fe Trail

Santa Fe, NM 87503
Tel.: (505) 827-7400
Toll Free: 1-800-545-2040
(For consumer materials)
1-800-545-2070
(For department)

**New York State Division of Tourism,
Department of Economic
Development**
One Commerce Plaza
Albany, NY 12245
Tel.: (518) 474-4116
Toll Free: 1-800-CALL-NYS

**North Carolina Division of Travel
and Tourism**
430 N. Salisbury St.
Raleigh, NC 27603
Tel.: (919) 733-4171
Toll Free: 1-800-VISIT-NC

**North Dakota Department of
Tourism**
Liberty Memorial Bldg.
604 E. Blvd.
Bismarck, ND 58505
Tel.: (701) 224-2525
Toll Free: 1-800-435-5663

**Ohio Division of Travel and
Tourism**
P.O. Box 1001
Columbus, OH 43266-0101
Tel.: (614) 466-8844
Toll Free: 1-800-BUCKEYE
(Continental U.S. and
all of Canada)

**Oklahoma Tourism & Recreation
Department, Travel and Tourism
Division**
500 Will Rogers Bldg.
DA92
Oklahoma City, OK 73105-4492
Tel.: (405) 521-3981
Toll Free: 1-800-652-6552
(Information requests only)

Oregon Economic Development
  Department, Tourism Division
775 Summer St., NE
Salem, OR 97310
Tel.: (503) 373-1270
Toll Free: 1-800-547-7842

Pennsylvania Office of Travel
  Marketing
Room 453, Forum Building
Harrisburg, PA 17120
Tel.: (717) 787-5453
Toll Free: 1-800-VISIT-PA
    (For ordering visitors guide only)
    (U.S. and Canada)

Rhode Island Tourism Division
7 Jackson Walkway
Dept. TIA
Providence, RI 02903
Tel.: (401) 277-2601
Toll Free: 1-800-556-2484

South Carolina Division of Tourism
Box 71
Columbia, SC 29202
Tel.: (803) 734-0122

South Dakota Department of
  Tourism
711 E. Wells Ave.
Pierre, SD 57501-3369
Tel.: (605) 773-3301
Toll Free: 1-800-SDAKOTA
    (1-800-732-5682)

Tennessee Department of Tourist
  Development
P.O. Box 23170
TNDA
Nashville, TN 37202
Tel.: (615) 741-2158

Texas Department of Commerce,
  Tourism Division
P.O. Box 12728
Austin, TX 78711-2728
Tel.: (512) 462-9191
Toll Free: 1-800-88-88-TEX

Utah Travel Council
Council Hall/Capitol Hill
Dept. TIA
Salt Lake City, UT 84114
Tel.: (801) 538-1030

Vermont Department of Travel &
  Tourism
134 State St.
Montpelier, VT 05602
Tel.: (802) 828-3236
Toll Free: 1-800-338-0189
    (Trade Only)

Virginia Division of Tourism
1021 East Cary St.
Dept. VT
Richmond, VA 23219
Tel.: (804) 786-4484
Toll Free: 1-800-VISIT-VA

Washington State Tourism
  Development Division
P.O. Box 42500
Olympia, WA 98504-2500
Tel.: (206) 586-2088 or
    (206) 586-2012
Toll Free: 1-800-544-1800

West Virginia Division of Tourism
  & Parks
2101 Washington St., East
Charleston, WV 25305
Tel.: (304) 348-2286
Toll Free: 1-800-225-5982

Wisconsin Division of Tourism
P.O. Box 7606
Madison, WI 53707
Tel.: (608) 266-2161
Toll Free: 1-800-372-2737 (In-State)
    1-800-432-TRIP (Out-of-State)

Wyoming Division of Tourism
I-25 at College Dr.
Dept. WY
Cheyenne, WY 82002
Tel.: (307) 777-7777
Toll Free: 1-800-225-5996

DISTRICT OF COLUMBIA

**Washington, DC, Convention and
  Visitors Association**
1212 New York Ave., NW, Suite 600
Washington, DC 20005
Tel.: (202) 789-7000
Toll Free: 1-800-422-8644

Index

**If you enjoyed *RVing Basics*,
you may be interested in these Ragged Mountain
Press and International Marine books.**

Prices are in U.S. dollars and are subject to change.

Hedgemaids and Fairy Candles:

The Lives and Lore of North American Wildflowers

Jack Sanders

"Hedgemaids and Fairy Candles is destined to become a classic in the nature literature of our continent. Rooted in personal experience and scientific fact, Sanders' writing is riveting. Now wildflowers truly have a champion." —Wildflower *magazine*

Sanders examines in depth the lives and lore of more than eighty of North America's most popular wildflowers, including the origins of their names, their place in history and literature, what uses ancient herbalists found for them, where they grow, and much more.

Paperbound, 240 pages, 95 illustrations, $14.95. Item No. 057233-X.

Bass on the Fly

A. D. Livingston, with a Foreword by Nick Lyons

"Not only is this the best intro to fly fishing for bass I know, it isn't a bad intro to fly fishing, period. It's salty and deep-Southern and anti-snobbish." —Fly Rod & Reel

Paperbound, 160 pages, 75 illustrations, $16.95. Item No. 038151-8.

Outboard Boater's Handbook:

Advanced Seamanship and Practical Skills

David R. Getchell, Sr., editor

"This is not only a good and readable addition to any maritime library, but a must for the outboard boatman who wants to extract maximum use and pleasure from his craft with minimum headaches." —Buffalo News

Aided by contributions from other experts, veteran outboard skipper David R. Getchell, Sr., offers a wealth of useful facts on camping, customizing, outfitting, engine troubleshooting, piloting, repairs, maintenance, and more.

Paperbound, 272 pages, 120 illustrations, $19.95. Item No. 023053-6.